A NEW THEATRE

A NEW THEATRE

Tyrone Guthrie

McGraw-Hill Book Company

NEW YORK   TORONTO   LONDON

Books by Tyrone Guthrie

A NEW THEATRE

A LIFE IN THE THEATRE

THEATRE PROSPECT

THREE PLAYS FOR THE MICROPHONE

TOP OF THE LADDER (a play)
With Robertson Davies

RENOWN AT STRATFORD

TWICE HAVE THE TRUMPETS SOUNDED

THRICE THE BRINDED CAT HATH MEWED

Library of Congress Catalog Card Number: 64-22458
FIRST EDITION
25301

Contents

A NEW
THEATRE

1

Breakfast and a Plan

This is the story of how a new enterprise came to be started. The plan was to found an institution, something more permanent and more serious in aim than a commercial theatre can ever be. It is too early to know whether this aim has been achieved; but the first steps have been successfully taken. This, however, is not intended to be a success story. I had determined to write the story, even if the endeavour had been a disastrous failure, because I think the reasons for starting it and the practical steps taken are worth recording.

Whether our enterprise eventually succeeds or fails—and I have little doubt that it will succeed—other similar attempts are certainly going to be made; and I hope that this account may be of some help to those who make them.

Our theatre opened to the public with a service of dedication on Sunday, May 5, 1963. On the following night a performance of **Hamlet** was given to an invited audience. The first public performance was on Tuesday, May the seventh.

That was the culmination of four and a half years' work.

In March 1959, Oliver Rea had asked Peter Zeisler and myself to breakfast at the Plaza Hotel, in New York. I knew Zeisler quite well. We had worked together on the production of Leonard Bernstein's and Lillian Hell-

man's musical version of **Candide;** I found something
very congenial in his hard-boiled, sardonic humour, and
the rather rare combination of a high degree of literacy
and sensitivity with solid professional competence. He
had achieved a considerable reputation in New York
as a stage director. A stage director is the head man of
the technical organisation of costumes, properties and
lighting; and, after the production has opened, for the
discipline backstage. It is a job which demands quick
thinking, a clear grip upon a formidable mass of detail,
much of it very boring, and a good deal of authority.

Oliver Rea I knew less well. My wife and I had
met him and his wife through our mutual friend Eileen
Herlie. We had liked them, been once or twice to their
home, but so far the connection had been no more than
pleasantly social.

The breakfast had a purpose which was more than
merely social. It was to propose an alliance and a plan.
The alliance made sense. We were to pool our theatrical experience, mine as a director, Zeisler's as a technician, Rea's as an entrepreneur, manager or producer
(the terms are all rather loose and meaningless, but
imply administrative rather than technical or artistic
services). The sum of our three experiences and skills
was more than three times the value of each singly.

The plan was more vague. All of us felt considerable dissatisfaction with the theatrical set-up as we
found it in New York, and for very similar reasons. But
dissatisfaction is a negative state of mind. About the
positive steps which we should take we were neither
clear nor unanimous.

I said that I could not talk seriously nor think clearly
in New York—too many distractions, too nervous an
atmosphere, far too many telephone calls. I suggested,

and the other two kindly agreed, that we should all try to do some thinking on our own and meet later in the year at my home in Ireland, which is in the depths of very remote country; and there, in quietude, try to formulate a plan.

Before going to Ireland I will try briefly to explain our dissatisfaction with New York.

2

Give My Regards to Broadway

In New York is concentrated virtually the entire professional theatre of the whole United States.

For about fifty years, since movies became a dominant medium of public entertainment, road business has been steadily declining. Touring is now rarely profitable unless there is the attraction of a great star's name, or unless the play has just been a "smash hit" in New York and has been continuously mentioned in the press and in private conversation for a year or more.

At the turn of the century every important city had its own resident stock company, many of excellent quality. I do not know of a single one still in existence. Now there are many summer theatres, most of them in or near holiday resorts, which offer for the most part a weekly "package." The package consists of one of the lightweight Broadway successes of yesteryear, with a "star"—not always quite of the first magnitude or in the full flush of success—supported by one or two seasoned players. The remaining roles are undertaken by apprentices, who also paint the scenery, wash the floors, and do, with widely different degrees of efficiency, the hundred and one chores involved in running a theatre. They do this for nothing; sometimes the parents even pay for the privilege of having their young so employed. Some of these apprentices are serious aspirants, more of them are doing it because it is great

fun and Mommy and Daddy are such bores. With a few
very honourable exceptions, the summer theatre is no
more than an upper-middle-class frivolity, with neither
artistic nor commercial significance.

There are, outside New York, only a very few
serious theatrical enterprises at professional level. And
in addition there are the Summer Festivals of Shakespeare, of which in the whole fifty states there are no
more than four or five; and to the very best of my
knowledge only one, that at Stratford, Connecticut, at
fully professional level.

Finally there is the so-called academic theatre.
Many universities offer courses in drama, and there are
many excellently equipped university theatres, better
equipped indeed than almost any of the professional
Broadway theatres. In general, however, the drama departments are lowly considered by the governing bodies
of universities and get very low allocations of money.
The shocking assumption is made that the departments'
productions must be self-supporting. This is in line with
two very common general assumptions: that drama is
at best a harmless leisure pastime for elderly ladies; at
worst it is a corrupt and licentious display. The second
assumption is that anything which fails to pay its own
way cannot possibly be any good. From this assumption
religion and scientific research are excepted. They do
not pay their own way but they are worth backing,
because they may possibly lead to valuable results,
here or hereafter.

In order to make ends meet, university drama departments are forced into the position of commercial
managers. They have carefully to offset productions of
Aeschylus or Claudel (both obvious poison at the box
office, but essential if the programme is to be anywhere

near a standard which might justify a university degree) with popular light comedies and even student performances of Broadway musicals.

I have heard a professor of drama, a most earnest and reputable person, defending the educational values of his production of **Brigadoon.** Every one of his arguments would equally have justified a visit by his students to a freak show or a whorehouse in Suez. Indeed the latter would offer an opportunity, which **Brigadoon** missed, to brush up on foreign languages and international relations.

For the last two or three decades, the academic theatre has been attempting to do a job which the professional theatre has failed to do: namely, to offer some kind of live drama in places and to people who would otherwise have had none. I applaud the attempt but I question its wisdom. Shoestring productions, with a drama professor directing student actors, do not seem quite the right attraction to lure the lost sheep back into the theatrical fold.

Further, I question the purpose of many of these drama departments. Their main object seems too often to be that of **teaching** people to **teach** drama, rather than just trying to interest them in drama. This seems to be American pragmatism run wild. It may arguably be better for universities to try to qualify young people for jobs, rather than to try, as European universities do, merely to open their minds to intellectual possibilities. But surely it is desirable that the jobs for which students are being qualified should be reasonably useful jobs.

I question the utility of turning out every year some thousands of young people who are qualified to teach drama, the overwhelming majority of whom are hoping to get onto the staff of a college, where they hope to teach succeeding, ever-multiplying thousands to teach drama. Does drama, as taught and learnt in these institutions, justify all the trouble and expense?

Inevitably, as the yearly thousands of drama teachers multiply, they will create, indeed are creating, a vested interest, which maintains passionately the usefulness of academic drama and sees nothing wrong with the almost complete divorce between the professional and the academic theatre.

I once lectured about the theatre at a large university. My lecture, which was public, was quite well attended. I daresay five hundred students were there. At one point, I asked those who had ever attended a professional theatrical performance to put up their hands. Five did so. I then asked those who were studying drama to put up their hands. About three hundred did so. At dinner afterwards I asked my host, the professor of English (drama at this university is a rather stagnant backwater of English Lit.) how many of his students annually went onto the professional stage. He thought for a moment. "In the last ten years," he said, "just one, thank God!" Adding, with a ferocious glitter of rimless glasses, "a woman, naturally."

I quote this incident not to discredit academic theatre, but only as an instance of the gulf which divides the academic from the professional. The gulf is widened by mutual jealousy. The professionals are apt to regard the academics, many of whom are most gifted and able men, as shirkers, who have chosen the ease, security and dignity of academic life because they have never had the courage to face the uncertainties and furious competition of the stage; and as humbugs, because they profess to teach what can only be truly learnt in the hard school of experience and in front of paying customers. The university men, on their side, weigh upon the vulgar and mercenary character of the professional theatre; they point out, and often with full justification, how great talents are coarsened and degraded when they are sold for money; the sordid pettiness of fighting for top billing or solo curtain calls; the selfishness, pathological exhibitionism and, above all, shocking overpayment of stars. Each side, in fine, concentrates upon the shortcomings and underestimates the merits of the other. Minimal attempts are made to bridge the gap and to seek for ways in which each side might be helpful and useful to the other.

Thus the professional theatre now operates almost exclusively in one tiny area of New York City. This concentration has brought about interesting and alarming results.

First, economic: everything has acquired an ininflated monetary value. Theatres have been steadily pulled down to make way for hotels and office buildings, which are thought to bring a better return on the real estate investment, and indeed do bring a better financial return. As the number of theatres steadily dwindles, so the demand for the use of those remaining increases. Rents are astronomical; the lessors can and do impose outrageous terms. It is, for example, usual to compel a tenant, if his takings drop below a certain percentage of capacity, to vacate the building. This means that a manager, however rich, however well disposed, simply cannot "nurse" a play which may have made a shaky start, but which he believes will eventually find a public.

This sort of economic pressure forces management to resort to any and every conceivable kind of insurance against failure. One of the commonest kinds of insurance is to employ popular and celebrated leading players. Consequently the services of the very limited number of such players are in tremendous demand. They ask and get, enormous salaries. Their salaries, though puny compared with those of television or movie stars, are none the less out of all reasonable proportion to the service which they offer to the community. An actor's pay ought not reasonably to be ten times that of a judge or twenty times that of an archbishop. Competition, however, is not so hot for judicial or archiepiscopal services.

The pressure of space in New York City is such that the workshops where scenery and costumes and properties are made are, like the theatres, rented at fantastic rates. The people who make costumes, scenery and properties, quite apart from the wages which they have to pay to their workpeople—which we shall discuss in a moment—have to cover enormous overheads for rent, light, heat, power, rates and insurance. These charges naturally govern the price of their merchandise. In addition, the speculative nature of all theatrical business, for example, the heavy risk of bad debts and constant likelihood of merchandise going suddenly out of vogue, causes them to require a far higher rate of profit than is expected in ordinary retail trade. Actors too have to charge high for their services, because of the casual and irregular nature of their employment, and because, like that of the dressmaker, their merchandise is apt to go suddenly out of vogue.

These are merely instances of the fantastic cost of theatrical production in New York, which could be multiplied and enlarged upon but only to reach the same conclusion: namely, that management now simply cannot afford to make long-term plans or to aim at anything other than a smash hit.

Since smash hits occur about one in relation to ten smash flops, it may rather readily be inferred that the so-called "commercial" theatre is anything but a commercial operation. Yet, so enormous are the financial profit and the prestige which accrue from a smash hit that it is still possible to raise literally tens of millions of dollars every season to keep the Broadway theatre going. But this is no longer a business in which wisdom, thrift and honesty eventually pay dividends. It is a fantastic, speculative game.

There are still wise, thrifty and honest producers, but they realize that they are merely croupiers; occasionally, and to a limited extent, they gamble with their own money; most of the chips which they manipulate are paid for by amateur speculators, dazzled by the glamour of the theatre, hopeful with the insane persistence of all gamblers that this time, against all the odds, they will pull off the grand coup.

Next let us consider Broadway from the actor's point of view. The first and most terrible fact is that, according to statistics issued by Equity, the actors' trade union, only one-quarter to one-third of their members are working at any given time.

In itself this is not so bad. The two-thirds to three-quarters who are unemployed in the theatre can model sweaters, address envelopes, sling hash—in short, do all the dreary part-time jobs which people have to do if a part of their time and a great deal of their endeavour is fixed upon some other goal. The terrible part is the dog-eat-dog competition which ensues when several hundred people are chasing one job; the having to be seen smartly dressed and gaily chattering at the right parties; the buttering-up of useful or important people; the coarsening and humiliating ordeal of being "looked over" by managements, as though you were, as indeed in a sense you are, being bought.

I have known a thousand applicants to be "auditioned" for less than a dozen vacancies in the chorus of a musical comedy.

The constant marvel is that, in spite of it all, actors are so generous to one another, sharing information about jobs, being genuinely glad when a friend gets the job which they would like to have had; so cheerful and merry; and so insanely enthusiastic about their horrible job; so humbly and genuinely eager to improve both as craftsmen and artists.

Every year dozens, perhaps hundreds, of stage-struck young people reach New York from Denver; Buffalo; Grovers Corners, North Dakota; Scrunchup, South Carolina; many of them beautiful or talented, every one as eager as all get-out. If they do land a job —and we know that the odds are heavily against their doing so—what happens? Either the play is a flop, in which case they are out of work again at the end of three or four performances, or else the play is a success and runs for two years. This is really the deadlier of the two alternatives, because our young aspirant's part is unlikely to be much more than a spit and a cough. There are limits to the amount of oneself which can be poured into a spit and a cough. After the thirtieth week of eight weekly performances, that limit is apt to have been passed. And nothing new is being learnt.

On the whole, these young people are very eager to learn. In their spare time they go to classes. They rent rat-infested dens and call them "studios" and practice there. But, though this is better than nothing, it is not what they need. What a young actor needs is to play a number of very various parts in the quickest possible succession, under experienced direction with an experienced company and before the public. This is exactly what Broadway no longer offers.

It is true that television does now offer a great deal of work which would not otherwise be available. But television for all its many advantages has two grave drawbacks; you are performing to microphone and camera, and only indirectly to your fellow-creatures; and there is no substitute for a live audience; a "studio audience" is not the same thing at all. Second, in television it is almost impossible for the small parts and the younger people not to be type-cast. If you look just like a clerk in a corner store you will be cast as a clerk in a corner store, and they will only send for you when a clerk in a corner store is called for in the script. Until you have in some way been able to prove your versatility, you will get no variety of parts; and television producers are not going to waste time and money training you to be versatile. It is cheaper and easier, and possibly even more efficient, to pick out of the countless throng of aspirants someone who seems to look and sound exactly like the part which has to be cast.

New York is crawling with acting schools and private teachers; some of them are excellent, most of them are ill-qualified humbugs, who are not ashamed to take fees from pupils too humble and too ignorant to expose them. Even the excellent ones cannot teach the lessons which can only be learnt, and often very painfully, by practical experience in front of an audience, composed not of friends, well-wishers and artistic aunts, but of the public. The public is a many-headed creature, which the actor must learn to subdue until it is as gentle and meek as a little pet lamb.

You can study the theory of lion-taming till you are blue in the face; you can pay people to teach you how to speak soothing, endearing words to the big cats, or how to beat the hell out of them with a whip; but you will not be a lion-tamer till you've been right into that cage a dozen times. If you have a talent for lion-taming your lessons won't take very long to learn; if you have no talent, it won't take very long for the lions to gobble you right up.

Finally, in this brief survey of the Broadway scene, let us consider the trade-union situation. The three unions most concerned are those of the actors, the stagehands and musicians. They came into being in order that their members might have the power of collective bargaining with those who wanted to hire them. They came into being to fight gross, cruel and long-endured abuse exercised by employers upon employed.

This must not be forgotten.

But tyranny begets tyranny. Abuse begets abuse. Now the officials of the unions have the whip-hand; and for years they have been getting in their licks not only at bad employers but at all employers; not only at employers but at their own members. Actors, musicians and stagehands are all so "protected" by their unions that they can hardly call their souls their own.

I am not going to embark upon a discussion of wage scales. It is too specialised; and who is to say what is the right wage for a small-part actor, a flautist at the back desk, or an individual whose sole duty is to carry a chair from one side of a stage to the other? The principle of agreed minimum salaries is right. What I cannot regard as anything but tyrannous is the principle that the union can dictate to an employer whom he may, or may not, hire; and worse still, that he cannot fire someone with whose services he is dissatisfied. What I cannot regard as anything but inefficient is the mass of doctrinaire regulations which assume that employers are always, and in every circumstance, the deadly enemies of the employed; and the implied tyranny by union officials, which makes the employees afraid to infringe even the pettiest of union rules.

I will give two instances of what I regard as union tyranny taken from my own experience. At one theatre in New York I directed a play in which neither scenery nor music were required. But their respective unions had "allotted" a minimum number of musicians and a minimum number of stagehands to this particular house. There was no argument; if the management wished ever to employ members of either union, they had no option but to submit to the unions' views about how many stagehands or musicians should comprise the minimum. So every night during the run of this particular play three musicians and a rather larger number of stagehands came to the theatre. Their way of passing the time was to play poker, for high stakes, and with an amount of noise which was frequently detrimental to the play but which the stage-manager had apparently no power to quell. This was annoying to the actors; a further cause of annoyance was the fact that these noisy and inconsiderate gamblers were being paid, naturally under union regulations, higher wages than all but the highest-paid actors. Morale in this theatre was consequently low. The house was divided against itself, and we have it on good authority that such houses will fall.

Another instance: under union regulations if any furniture, properties or lights are used at rehearsals, a property master and an electrician and a carpenter must be employed for a minimum of four hours. Otherwise rehearsals must take place with the aid of one small table and a few bent-wood chairs. The stage may be lit only by a work light—a single, powerful, unshaded lamp, which does just enable the actors with inconvenience to read their scripts but in which the expression of their faces cannot be seen, and which, because of its glaring and unshaded beam, ensures that everyone, after an hour or two, will have a splitting headache. Rehearsals in such conditions are extremely inefficient. Yet it is strictly forbidden to bring in some suitable furniture and a few light properties which the actors and stage-management could easily, and would willingly, handle. It is strictly forbidden to use any comfortable and efficient source of light, though this could easily be arranged by touching a single switch. Managements must either pay about $500 a week for the services of three quite unnecessary men, or endure the prescribed conditions, which are deliberately made inefficient and uncomfortable as a lever to force the employment of union men. And this kind of "featherbedding" is not to protect a group of weak and defenceless workers. It is in the interest of skilled and highly paid specialists. Nor is there grave unemployment amongst members of this union. It is now extremely hard to recruit an intelligent and able-bodied crew. The television studios get the pick of the union men, because the hourly rates are higher and there is apt to be more overtime. The theatre takes the people whom the union sends; and it is highly impolitic to raise the least objection.

Operator 64
373-2668
Mr. Miller
Minneapolis

Note
33 8 - 111 ✓

Perhaps it should also be stated that entry into this union is extremely restricted; that, in itself, is not necessarily objectionable. It is, however, objectionable if good men are refused permission because the limited number of places has been filled by sons, friends and hangers-on of those who already hold union cards.

At present all the claims and regulations of these unions are based solely on protecting and advancing the sectarian interest of their own members. They are selfish and short-sighted and, in the long run, if they do not change their attitude they will kill the goose which lays the golden eggs. They not only make management even more expensive and speculative than it already is; more serious, they take the joy out of the work. One of the charms of the theatre is that it is a co-operative art: the author is dependent upon his interpreters; they, in turn, upon others, carpenters, electricians, dress-makers, hairdressers, flymen; and all are dependent upon the public.

The tyranny of the unions has to a great extent destroyed all feeling of unanimous effort backstage. How can actors feel warmly towards stagehands and musicians, whose union **compels** them to put their own sectarian interest ahead of that of the show, no matter who suffers? How can producers feel warmly towards actors, whose union **compels** them to insist on the fulfillment to the letter of every petty regulation, no matter how inconvenient or expensive such insistence can be?

And, finally, how long can a theatre endure which largely, though not entirely, because of union demands is steadily pricing itself out of reach of any but rich people?

That brings me to the final aspect of Broadway,

which led me and my partners to go elsewhere: the audience.

The high cost of rents, production material and wages must inevitably be passed on to the customer. Ticket prices are now such as to discourage the habit of regular theatregoing. More and more, audiences have ceased to be made up of families or parties of ordinary people, celebrating Jack's engagement or Aunt Lou's birthday. Too expensive. Now, more and more, audiences are composed of very rich, elderly people, of tourists and of business men and women entertaining other business men and women on expense accounts. Few of these people are regular theatregoers, interested in the art of the theatre, who can criticise knowledgeably and distinguish merit from success. The excitement of success is what the new audience desires above all, and for this it is willing to pay dearly. Hence the hit almost automatically becomes the super-smash hit; and for the same reason the flop is flop-total. It is not wholly the expense of management which makes moderate success impossible. The new Broadway public is not content with moderate success; that is not sufficiently exciting. Consequently there is no room for the play of solid merit, which **a priori** cannot have massive popular appeal. Appetite grows by what it feeds on. Each year David Merrick's ballyhoo grows more cynically, successfully and vulgarly sensational. This is not a vulgar man: it is a man with a detached and Oriental sense of humour, whom it amuses to play the public as an angler plays a fish. Each year the public rises to a gaudier, more garish and more deadly bait.

Policy in the theatre demands continuity of aim and consistency of style. Without a policy, no theatre can possibly create its **own** public; and unless it does so,

it is compelled to surrender to the kind of policy which
Mr. Merrick's management exemplifies: the pursuit of
the smash hit at any cost.

Only three theatres in New York even profess a
policy: the Metropolitan Opera House, the City Center
and the Repertory Theatre of Lincoln Center. You may
fault the Met for many things; but it cannot be denied
that the management there is consistent. It is doing its
utmost to achieve something supremely difficult. The
main criticism which I hear levelled at the Met is that
it is trying to blow upon the embers of a dead fire; that
nothing new or daring is ever tried there. I see nothing
wrong with presenting the greatest singers of the day
in inevitably imperfect, but rarely contemptible, productions of well-tried favourites. "Experiment" with the
greatest singers of our own or any other day is unthink-
able, not merely financially but psychologically. The
aura of the Met is inevitably grand, rather than exciting.
One need not expect that the Great, the Arrived, will
be exciting. Nevertheless there should be a grand, distinguished crimson and gold opera house in every
civilised metropolis. To expect it also to be "exciting" is
as silly and unreasonable as to expect that the Board
of General Motors should all be as dazzling as Rudolph
Valentino.

The City Center can afford to be, and is, more experimental. And here is the one theatre in New York
that has achieved a regular audience, to be part of
which one feels proud, happy and stimulated. As at the
Old Vic in its palmy days, the goings-on are sometimes
incommensurate with the enthusiasm. But how indispensable is enthusiasm to the enjoyment of any public
occasion.

Then there is the Lincoln Center Repertory Theatre. It is still too early to make judgements. But clearly this is an attempt to implement a policy, to substitute long-term for short-term views. Therefore, as with our own project in Minneapolis, it must be allowed time to mature, to survive inevitable growing pains. Until more productions have been seen, it is not possible to assess either the theories which the policy expresses or the way in which they have been put into practice. Can the high aims of the directors resist the almost irresistible pressure with which New York pushes its theatre towards a kind of success which can be measured in dollars?

As yet it is only possible to wish well to the new venture and to applaud the courage which aims higher than the smash hit.

How do you achieve a smash hit? Is it a matter of spontaneous combustion, a delicious explosion when play hits inflammable audience? Just now and again it is. More often it is a deliberate contrivance of saleable elements, which are then offered at bargain rates to the arrangers of theatre parties.

The theatre party is one of the best business ideas which ever backfired to the jeopardy of the American theatre. Management sells a large block of seats, sometimes the whole house, to a battleaxe in Mineola or White Plains. She then rallies her forces and sells the seats to her friends at a profit. Usually this is done in aid of a charity, and I have known a whole house to be sold out at fifty dollars a head. The audience, which feels that it has been shanghaied by the battleaxe, assembles in a towering rage. At fifty bucks they feel that they owe nothing to the performance, not even attention.

Theoretically, it should be a splendid idea to sell the entire house to a homogeneous party, so that play-going becomes, as it always should be, a sociable event; and the audience becomes, as it always should be, a group of friends assembled to enjoy an experience together, and then, in addition, some charity gets a nice little contribution, a thank-offering as it were, from happy audience, happy management and happy battle-axe.

In practice, it goes wrong, partly because the financial side gets out of hand; the whole thing becomes an outrageous, extortionate racket; and partly because the sorts of people who are good at organising, canvassing and accounting are not very good at assessing beforehand either the tastes of their clients or the quality of a production, especially when the latter has to be determined almost entirely by the celebrity of those concerned. Theatre party organisa-tions can, and do, ensure that **Camelot** or **Sound of Music** will open to advance bookings of millions of dollars, by which they are assured of a run of several years. This is economically convenient; but it implies that the way to attract theatre parties is not to create a good entertainment, but to create an entertainment which, on paper, looks, before it opens, as though it were likely to be good—Mary Martin, Richard Burton, Lerner and Lowe, Rogers and Hammerstein, Jerome Robbins, Oliver Smith. But, as any housewife knows, luscious ingredients do not of themselves make a good meal; they must be judiciously mixed and lovingly cooked.

Further, the kind of entertainments to which party organisers are attracted are of the kind which least require their assistance. Theatre parties are of virtually no assistance in the promotion of the "difficult," "unusual," potentially serious kind of productions, to which their patronage would be economically and socially important, which would make their patronage artistically significant. I am well aware that party organisers are not in business for the benefit of the theatre; they are using the theatre as a means of raising money for charity. It should, theoretically, be possible for the interest of the theatre and of the charities to coincide. Unhappily, theatre party organisations, like so much else in the Broadway complex, have allowed artistic significance to be overshadowed by a greedy, short-term attitude towards money-making.

What about that complex of activity which is known as "off-Broadway"? I cannot see how off-Broadway productions are in a position to avoid the dangerous pressures which bedevil Broadway. You can present a play off-Broadway on a lower budget, but you are still paying exorbitant, albeit slightly less exorbitant, prices for rent, goods and services, and your possibilities of profit are more than correspondingly less.

In my view the only way that off-Broadway could really become a valuable supplement to Broadway would be if it were conducted as an amateur operation —for Love, not Money. Now, however, with a very few shining and honourable exceptions, it is amateurishly professional. In dingy conditions, which we all try to glorify as "intimate," productions are cheaply, and too often incompetently, mounted of plays which are no more adventurous or interesting than those which Broadway is presenting.

For it is a fact that, however one feels about

Broadway, each season an extraordinary variety and range of drama finds its way onto the stage. The whole system may be faulted for lack of policy, for too much concern with monetary success, for this and for that. It cannot be faulted for lack of an adventurous, enthusiastic, inquisitive spirit.

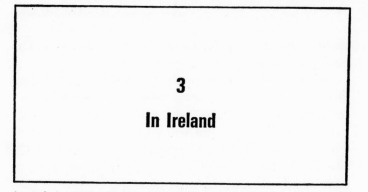

3
In Ireland

In July, 1959, the Reas and the Zeislers arrived to visit with us in Ireland. It was Irish midsummer weather; which is to say that, day after day, clouds, like damp, dark-grey tulle, enveloped the house, the landscape, ourselves, in warm, soft, permeating vagueness.

This weather is the cause of Ireland's glories and her miseries. It is relaxing. It is conducive to gentle, melancholy meditation. It is supremely non-conducive to strenuous physical, mental or moral effort. It induces late rising—who wants to get out of a warm bed and put on damp underclothes in a damp, twilit bedroom? It induces long, lazy, philosophic or reminiscent talks over the ruins of breakfast. It induces anecdotage. It induces alcoholism. And all this induces a great, an overwhelming, consciousness of sin in Catholic and Protestant breasts alike. In the forefront of the catalogue of sin stand the sins of the flesh; and at their head, of course, stands sexual sin.

But in Ireland every pleasure, not just the carnal joys but even the most harmless and infantile indulgence, has a great load of sin hung about its poor neck. This, not poverty, is the root of our addiction to dreary cooking, dreary clothes, dreary houses filled with dreary furniture. To have houses, clothes or meals which were a cause of pleasure would be sinful. Who would risk an

33

eternity of torturing flames for the sake of a gay hat,
new curtains or a potted shrimp?

But this dreariness, again, provokes reaction. Can
there be any other country where conversation and
repartee are so skilfully merry? Where a funeral is so
madly gay? Where what you might call the poetry of
idle and shiftless living is so graceful and gentle? Or
where sex, driven ferociously underground, explodes in
such weird, unexpected, even alarming contexts?

It is foolish to generalise about national charac-
teristics. People obviously are not of such or such a kind
simply because they live in a part of the map which is
coloured green or yellow or red; but climate, environment and history do affect character. Americans, accustomed to a considerable standardisation of environment, must surely be amazed at the notable differences
of climate and landscape between England and Ireland,
though there is less than a hundred miles between them;
and still more at the differences between English and
Irish people—a difference of appearance and dialect
which no one can miss, and, more important, a difference in outlook, which is the result of history. Irishmen
feel a strong resentment towards the larger and more
powerful community, which, often quite unconsciously,
has done much to subject and injure the smaller, weaker
neighbour. Thus England has earned envy and dislike,
so that even her acts of neighbourly kindness and generosity are suspect.

Englishmen are naïvely wounded and provoked by
this Irish attitude. They cannot understand how inevitable it is for the poor to envy the rich, the weak to
envy the strong, and to resent kindness and generosity
because they suspect pity and reject patronage.

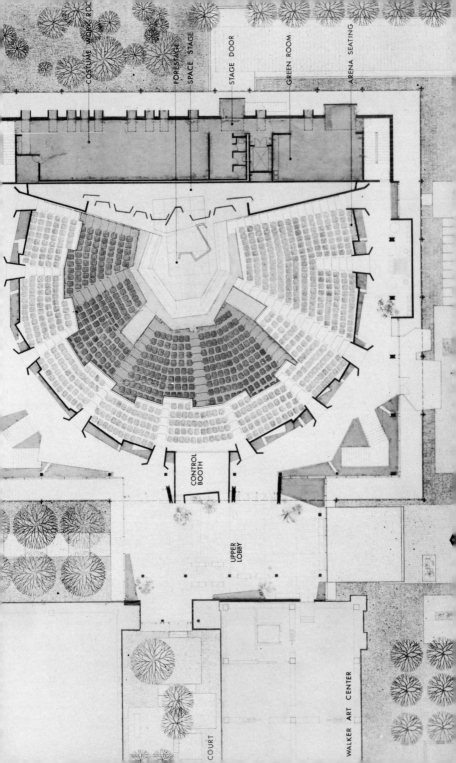

COSTUME WORK ROO

FORESTAGE

SPACE STAGE

STAGE DOOR

GREEN ROOM

ARENA SEATING

CONTROL
BOOTH

UPPER
LOBBY

COURT

WALKER ART CENTER

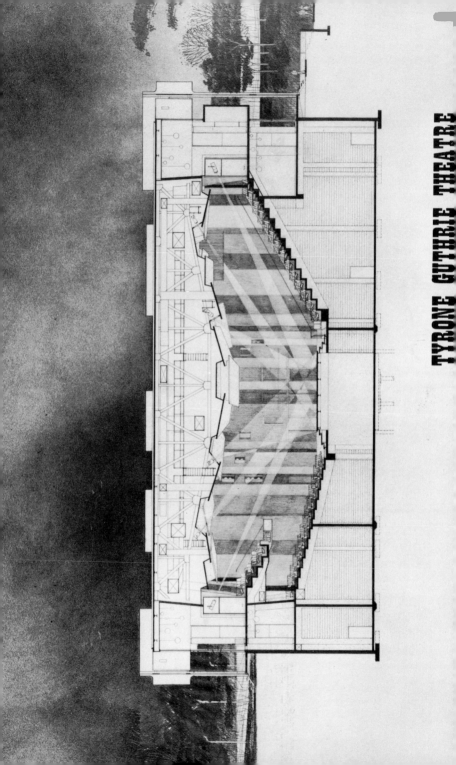

TYRONE GUTHRIE THEATRE

Americans are now the rich and powerful neighbours of Europe. Anxious to be kind and neighbourly, desperately anxious to be liked, they are naïvely wounded and provoked by the European attitude of "Yankee Go Home"; they resent the fact that Europeans accept their money but also reject their friendship. In the long course of time the balance will be adjusted. Eventually it will be America's turn to be poorer and weaker than an overwhelming neighbour—the Chinese, maybe, or the Men from Mars. Then Americans will feel the burning anger and resentment with which the kind neighbourly acts of the well-heeled neighbour have always been, and always will be, met.

Long talks over the ruins of breakfast; long talks crouched over the fire at night; long talks up to the neck in damp raspberry canes or bent double over the chickweed; long talks hacking at the overgrown rhododendrons, no less prolific than the chickweed . . . gradually we began to arrive at A Plan.

At first we had thought along the lines of a "Mid-Atlantic" company, which should produce a vague sort-of-a-something called Good Plays, in London where costs are lower, and bring them to New York, where takings can be higher. But pretty soon this plan appeared to be financially unfeasible and artistically nebulous. Also, we were none of us eager to work in New York; and I, for my part, felt rather unattracted to London.

I felt that over the years I had made what contribution I could offer to the London theatre. I had directed opera at Covent Garden and at Sadler's Wells; I had directed Shakespeare—twenty of his plays—at the Old Vic and Stratford-upon-Avon, many twice and some three times; I had been Administrator of the Old Vic and Sadler's Wells; I had directed many "commercial" plays in the West End; and many "experimental" plays in possibly more interesting and certainly less remunerative circumstances. I felt no urge for my own pleasure, still less as a public duty, to go on doing the same sort of thing.

On the other hand, I did feel very much attracted to some kind of a theatrical project aimed at those parts of the United States into which Broadway's influence did not penetrate. This seemed to be something potentially useful, a contribution worth trying to make. It was also something which I found very congenial.

My partners, without me, would have found it difficult, as Americans, to get permission to work in London; and gradually they too began to get bitten with the missionary bug, to want to start a professional theatre where it would be filling a need, rather than to be one more minnow in the already crowded fish tanks of Broadway and the West End.

Partly we were actuated by missionary zeal; but common sense also told us that the laws of supply and demand had better not be overlooked. It was clear that London and New York were not merely adequately supplied with theatrical enterprise, they were grossly over-supplied.

It was also clear that, with the exception of five or six cities which were used for the "tryouts" of Broadway productions, and with the exception of Chicago, every other city in the United States was grossly undersupplied. It was not, however, clear whether all these cities regarded this as a deprivation; whether, in fact, they were not entirely content to remain in a theatrical Sahara, entirely content with what they had—movies, TV, amateurs working with high aspirations and low budgets, and rather grubby little shows in dark night-clubs.

The next practical step seemed clear: to try to find out which cities, if any, would welcome a serious theatre and would offer it both financial and moral support.

Before taking this step, we felt that we had better know more clearly just what sort of a theatre we had in mind. It might, before the Plan became a reality, be necessary greatly to modify any conception at which we should now arrive. But we had better, we felt, **have** a conception, and a pretty clearly considered one, before anyone suggested modifications.

I have seen too many well-intentioned theatrical projects fail. The reefs upon which they have been wrecked have nearly always been the same; too unambitious a budget and too vague a policy.

Clearly, before you make a budget you must have a policy which the budget is intended to implement. Such a policy is useless if it cannot be clearly explained in, at most, four short simple sentences which anyone of reasonable intelligence can immediately understand. Most theatrical policies are neither explained, nor indeed explicable. But then most theatres try to operate without a policy.

Most of the well-intentioned projects aim to do Good Plays as well as their budgets will allow. But the term Good Plays is never defined. Perhaps this is just as well, because I suspect that it is indefinable. In fact, it usually boils down to meaning plays which the management admires. All too often the management's taste is not immediately endorsed by the public. Then, as the coffers empty, panic sets in and plays are chosen for production from all sorts of categories, be-

cause—so the management rationalizes its decisions—
they are "good of their kind." Then **Macbeth** is followed
by **Private Lives; Oedipus Rex** jostles with **Three Men on
a Horse;** new plays of promise are "balanced" by old
plays of repute; nobody—neither management, actors
nor audience—knows what they are trying to achieve,
nor what the hell is the score.

Another and more clear-cut and definable policy is
to aim at "success." There is only one objective method
of measuring success: count the takings at the box
office. The play with the highest takings is the biggest
success. You buy "properties" (these sorts of plays are
always known as properties. The term is intended to be
complimentary.) which have, if possible, shown themselves to have "smash-hit potentiality." The transatlan-
tic planes are bursting with producers trying to best
David Merrick in the acquisition of properties which
have been smash hits in London, Paris, Berlin or—good
heavens, this is business not pleasure—in places no one
has ever heard of, like Athens or Dublin. You then "put
the property on" with the best possible insurance which
star names can provide, strictly type-cast of course—
who wants to see Bette Davis except in a Bette Davis
part?—then, if the property is a smash hit, it makes a
simply colossal killing. If it's **not** a smash hit, you roll up
your sleeves, spend a fortune on promotion with the
idea of convincing everyone that it **is.** Even if you don't
convince **everyone,** you can certainly, by spending
enough, by talking their own language, convince that
bunch of cynical simpletons known collectively as the
film industry. By selling the film rights you can recover
what you've spent on the promotion and a sizeable part
of the original investment in the property.

As a policy this may not take a very long-sighted

or idealistic view of a producer's responsibility. But it is consistent; it is honest in theory, though not quite always in practice; it can be stated in one sentence of twelve short words: "Aim for a smash hit all the time and at any cost." These words are not only short, they are universally intelligible because they apply to an alarmingly high proportion of all human efforts in all spheres, in all parts of the world and at all times.

We rejected both these two possible policies. The smash hit policy we rejected partly because we did not admire or want that sort of success; and certainly in my own case, and I suspect that of my partners, we did not think we had the single-minded, ruthless drive which is necessary to achieve it. About the Good Play policy we were dubious because it was too vague and because it had caused the shipwreck of so many worthy enterprises. All the same, we thought it might be all right. First, if we could find an intelligible way of defining "good"; second, having found such a definition, could raise enough capital to stick to our policy, if at first it was not popular, for long enough to give it a chance of finding a public. "Long enough" seemed to us to be at least three seasons. Therefore the first clear thing to emerge was that we must think of this as being at least a three-year plan.

A theatre, like any other business, depends upon collecting the kind of customer who wants to buy the particular kind of article which you are selling. One of the drawbacks to Broadway is that, with the exception of the Met and the City Center, none of the theatres is catering for a particular public. They are all aiming merely to attract as many customers as possible. Their policy, if you can call it a policy, is to hope that every offering may be enormously popular and to assure the public that it is so. The prohibitive cost of management in New York does not make it possible for a policy gradually and steadily to establish itself. Yet the only way to restore the theatre to health is, in our opinion, to establish a policy and gradually to collect a public which will support it. The process must inevitably be gradual since the public will not be immediately aware of the policy, and cannot immediately determine whether to support it or not.

Now came the matter of defining what is a "good" play. No one knows what will be a good play until it has been tried. All too often, scripts which seemed excellent when read have turned out poorly when performed. Sometimes this is due to miscasting or misdirection. The fact remains that if anyone knew for certain just by reading it whether a play were good—not necessarily successful or popular, just good—he would be possessed of an insight never before known to man. We would also be richer than Croesus and Midas rolled into one.

It is, however, possible to know which plays have, in the past and by several generations of good judges, been considered good. Sometimes success has been ephemeral—great contemporary success is usually, though not always, ephemeral. All works of art, even the greatest, go through a period when they are out of popular favour. This usually occurs between twenty and fifty years after a work was first created, when the children of the artist's own generation are growing up, and for the thirty years or so when **their** taste is predominant. Children nearly always, as they grow up, react strongly against the taste of their parents. I belong to a generation which reacted violently against the British cult of Kipling, against realistic painting, against

Brahms and Wagner and mid-nineteenth-century church music. Some of the things which my parents admired and which my generation decisively rejected are gone forever. Others are creeping back into favour. Kipling is likely to be a classic; our disapproval did not greatly injure Brahms; about Wagner I am not so sure. Gradually the works of art which are destined to become "classical," begin to assert themselves. The cultural grain remains on the threshing floor; the chaff is winnowed away.

It seemed to us that the only way of knowing a good play from a bad was to apply the test of time. Our programme would be classical; only those plays would be chosen which had seemed, to discriminating people for several generations, to have serious merit; which had, in fact, withstood the test of time. This would still offer a very wide choice.

We could define our policy still more precisely. We would each season offer not merely a series of classics, but of classics which in origin, style and content would contrast interestingly one with another, would pose the implicit question: what is a classic and what has made it so?

Now the American theatre has not been long enough in existence to have developed its own classics. A distinctively American, as opposed to merely English-speaking, theatre only began to develop around the end of the First World War, at the beginning of the nineteen-twenties. Before that there certainly had been plays, written by American authors for American audiences, such as the works of Clyde Fitch. These, however, were heavily derivative from European and, naturally enough, especially from English-speaking sources.

Eugene O'Neill was the first distinctively American

playwright of importance. I believe that his ponderously repetitive style, his limited vocabulary and occasional **very** purple patches will ultimately keep him out of a place anywhere near the first rank. But his place in dramatic history is secure. So, in the more limited field of theatrical (as opposed to dramatic) history, is that of the Theatre Guild, which was during the next quarter-century (1920-45) to do more than any other management to establish indigenous drama in the United States.

If it be granted that fifty years is the absolute minimum of time required before a new work of art can wisely be regarded as a classic, then it follows that the American theatre cannot as yet claim to have developed a classical dramatist.

All the same, many excellent dramatists have developed between 1920 and the present time. Several of these, it is reasonable to suppose, may be of potential classical status. In planning a theatre which we hoped to establish in an American city, and hoped might have a perceptible cultural influence in a particular region of America, it seemed neither sensible nor tactful to take such a doctrinaire view of classical status that American plays would have—for at least another ten years—to be omitted from the programme.

Moreover, Americans get exasperated by Europeans who point out how brief American history has been. That it is true does not make a fact more agreeable. Europeans use the seniority of their culture to give maddening little lectures intended of course for the betterment and instruction of a crude, young and, of course, **totally** materialistic society. The British, I am afraid, are the very worst offenders. We use the fact that Britain and America write a similar language, and that the British have been writing for a few centuries longer, to take an absurdly patronising attitude towards our young cousins, not only in cultural matters but in everything where so-called "maturity" of outlook and behaviour might be valuable.

We certainly did not want it to appear as if once again Britain were trying to instruct the colonists. It therefore seemed to us essential to include each season one American play of what we considered to be potential classical status; and to let it take its place in a programme of established classics.

Before we leave the topic of Anglo-American relations: although we Limeys are frequently maddening in our assumption of superiority—and this is not less maddening because it is usually quite unconscious—yet Americans can sometimes be maddening too. I am repeatedly told, and I believe it is intended as a compliment, that my "British dialect" is cute; my spelling is constantly being corrected: theatre to "theater," colour to "color," night to "nite." Each of these instances, and each of a hundred others which I could enumerate, is utterly trivial and casts not the least shadow over the affection and admiration which I feel for hundreds of Americans. But it has been the years when I have enjoyed the boundless hospitality and generosity of this marvellous country, which have given me a new and more sympathetic understanding of Ireland's ungenerous, unintelligent and utter rejection of all things English, even English magnanimity.

It may be more blessed to give than to receive. But, for the poorer partner anyway, it is infinitely more difficult to receive.

By the time the Reas and Zeislers returned to sunshine from our misty shores, A Plan was under way.

4

Who'll Buy My Lavender?

A month or two after our meeting in Ireland we were all back in New York. We were agreed as to the general conception of our theatre; a classical programme, of which about one play in four should be an American play of potential classic status; this to be offered to any city which felt deprived of live theatre and would take us under its wing.

Did such a city, or cities, exist? We knew that most of the cities of America had virtually no live theatre. Maybe they preferred to have none. How should we find out?

We decided to consult Brooks Atkinson, who was then the critic of "The New York Times." We all knew him slightly, admired immensely his absolute integrity as a critic, and his disinterested enthusiasm for the theatre. This enthusiasm, you might think, would be dampened by many years as a critic. At first, yes; for the first year or so, maybe the first five years, you might be able to go to a play four of five nights a week and still retain some freshness, some of the eagerness with which you embarked on the job. Atkinson had been at it for four times five years and still, in a hard-boiled, not at all naïve, way was stage-struck.

On one of those matchless, golden, New York days of late September we lunched in Dinty Moore's. Atkinson, with his intelligent, quizzical hedgehog's face, listened as we expounded our plan and the reasons which underlay its conception.

He didn't say much; but allowed us to see that he thought our hearts were in the right place, even if there were something wrong with our heads. He said he would mention the plan on the drama page of "The New York Times." Something might come of it; you never know. He would also send us a list of plays which, in his opinion, had been somewhat overlooked and might be worth considering.

A shrewd, sensible, helpful list of plays arrived next morning. A day or two later a paragraph appeared in the "Times," briefly summarising the plan, mentioning our various qualifications to operate it and wondering whether there might be any takers.

It would be nice to be able to tell how the United States Mail was totally inundated by the avalanche; how a specially recruited force of secretaries waded waist-deep in a sea of paper; how each letter, more emotional than the last, implored us to found our theatre in the writer's home-town. But strict truth compels us to face the fact that the grand total of applications for our services was seven. But quality compensated for quantity. They were sensible and realistic.

Oliver Rea replied to them all that we were happy to hear of their interest, would visit their city on such-and-such a date and would our correspondent please arrange for us to meet the widest possible cross-section of interested people or groups in his community.

Peter Zeisler, then stage director of **The Sound of Music,** could not leave New York. Oliver, my wife and myself, equipped with spears and blowpipes, with pretty beads, bright shells and jews' harps to bribe the native chieftains, took the plane to Boston.

Dr. Abram L. Sachar, president of Brandeis Uni-

versity, was interested in the possibility of our directing
a resident professional company on his campus. Money
had been bequeathed for a theatre; we should have
some voice in the design.

The offer was an extremely generous one. We expressed our gratitude, explained that we had been ap-
proached by several other communities and must
explore the whole situation before making a decision.

The next port of call was San Francisco. Our contacts here were charming but vague. We met the mayor,
who thought we had come to promote the sale of Irish
whiskey; we met various groups of the citizenry, who
were polite but not very interested. We viewed something called the Cow Palace, and the site of some long-
ago Exposition, with Greek-style temples of crumbling
plaster which looked as though they had been designed
by Orson Welles for a scene which was subsequently
cut out of **Citizen Kane.** We visited two semi-profes-
sional groups operating semi-permanently in semi-
theatres. They too were polite, but obviously interested
in consolidating their own position rather than in the
somewhat different project with which we were concerned. We visited Mr. Louis Lurie, grand old theatre-
man of the Pacific coast. In a penthouse with Chinese
décor he offered us a spanking supper, served by an
"inscrutable" Oriental servant, who made us feel like
alley cats being given our milk by a pedigree Siamese.
Mr. Lurie would have been interested, I suspect, in dis-
cussing sharing terms in one of his theatres for a
bang-up revival of **The King and I,** with Richard Burton
and Elizabeth Taylor. At the mention of classical rep he
looked vaguely, though charmingly, into the far, far
distance and, opening a tiny cabinet, asked if we were
interested in Ming.

The next day, after a gracious luncheon on a

sunny patio enclosed by rose trellises . . . did we really
eat lotuses floating in myrrh? . . . we flew to Chicago.
There the temperature was zero. He-men in snow-
covered parkas, their huge faces mottled blue and
purple with the cold, stamped about and yelled "This
way to the helicopter."

Still in a dream of sun-drenched lotus petals, we
found ourselves on something called The Tarmac, in the
teeth of a wind which had screamed across the prairies
straight from the North Pole. The he-men bundled us
into a contrivance which looked a cross between a tea-
pot and Cinderella's pumpkin—the three of us and two
businessmen with briefcases. The door of the pumpkin
was slammed, a frail little door with a window which
let up and down like the windows of my grandfather's
brougham. Then to our naïve amazement the pumpkin
began to whirr and rose from the ground, straight up
into the falling snow. The businessmen, whose names
were Mulloy and O'Hara (I read the labels on their
briefcases), fell to their knees and besought the Holy
Virgin to bring them safely back to land. O'Hara leaned
towards me, the voice a fluty tenor, the accent Mul-
lingar-Bronx straight out of old-time vodavil: "Yez'll
pordon os. Mebbe we're an itty-bitty norvous."

An itty-bitty! . . . miserable pair of sissies! Ugh!
Faugh! Peugh! At that moment we grazed a factory
chimney; swerving to miss another, the pumpkin tipped
up sideways. I fell against the frail little door and
thought I felt the latch giving. With a scream I clutched
O'Hara, who was clutching Mulloy, who was clutching
the luggage rack.

My wife and Oliver sat bolt upright, mouths primly
pursed. "Faugh!" they seemed to be thinking, and
"Peugh" and "Ugh!"

Another and more violent lurch knocked the Ulster Presbyterian nonsense out of them. All five of us were now on the floor.

Ten minutes later we reached our destination, another airport in another part of the forest. A second lot of he-men in parkas opened the door. It was not till we saw the amazement writ on their mottled blue and purple faces, not till they exclaimed "Peugh" and "Faugh," that we realised that the five of us were sitting on the floor, holding hands and shrieking with maniac laughter. The Parkas thought they had opened a cage of drunken hyenas. Mebbe we were an itty-bitty norvous.

Another hour in another plane brought us to Minneapolis. Here the temperature was not zero but thirty degrees below zero, and the snow was thrice as deep. The wind at Chicago screamed and whistled. At Minneapolis it was silent, but you felt that a sharp, bright sword had pierced your bowels through and through.

To meet us came Frank Whiting, the head of the Drama Department at the University of Minnesota. He looks refreshingly unlike a professor; nor is he typecast as a thespian. You might take him for a vet; or a rather senior instructor in physical training; or maybe a brisk engineer, just off to supervise the Bridge over the River Kwai or a new dam in the Tennessee Valley.

What with the changes of temperature, the lotus luncheon, the screams in the helicopter, we were not unwilling, as the writers of manly travel stories say, to hit the sack.

Next day betimes splendid Frank Whiting was at the hotel. In sparkling sunshine and Frank's car we did a quick once-over of the Twin Cities.

Frank may not look like a professor but he drives

like one. On broad, straight, empty roads, he would creep along, scowling with intense concentration. In dense traffic he would roar round corners, telling stories, making jokes, pointing with one hand at objects of interest while blowing his nose with the other. All the same we covered a good deal of ground, geographically and in conversation. We saw the prim Episcopalian Cathedral of St. Mark — North Oxford in the upper Midwest; the gaily rococo Roman Catholic Cathedral of St. Mary — Vienna with more than a dash of Armagh; the Catholic Cathedral of St. Paul, which is claimed to be a replica, on a much smaller, scale of St. Peter's, Rome. Be this as it may, it is a handsome building, marvellously situated on a bluff overlooking the Mississippi River. But the river itself was what most charmed and amazed us. It had not yet frozen over and was flowing with a lively sparkle through winding gorges which are still beautiful, although here, as everywhere else, the convenience of the waterway has been exploited in the interests of trade. The banks are the usual mess of factories, coal dumps, freight yards, gasworks and power stations. Of course it will not always be so. Eventually the Twin Cities will realise that their river can be, and ought to be, a wonderful and life-giving amenity without losing any of its utility. It has taken London two thousand years even to begin to appreciate this about the Thames; it would therefore be unreasonable to expect that, after a mere hundred years, the Twin Cities should be making the most of the Mississippi.

In conversation we gathered something about the workings of the university's Drama Department; something about Frank himself; though he was entirely discreet, and some inkling began to dawn of some of the politics in which we should have to be involved. One thing was clear: Frank was determined that we should come to the Twin Cities.

We had another Minneapolitan contact. A month or so earlier Oliver and Betty Rea had spent a social weekend in Des Moines. A fellow-guest, a cousin of their host, had been John Cowles, Jr., vice-president of the "Minneapolis Star and Tribune," the leading newspaper in this part of the world. Oliver had discussed our project with Cowles, mentioning that, at the invitation of Professor Whiting, we should be visiting Minneapolis and canvassing support; Cowles promised to do what he could.

We lunched in an upper chamber at the newspaper office, where Cowles had invited a distinguished and influential group to meet us. We made our pitch. The group expressed polite but guarded interest. We departed to see the mayor.

I cannot remember all the calls which we made, nor the order in which they occurred. It has all become a slightly feverish blur. There were drinks with the members of Frank Whiting's staff, the Drama Department of the university. We assembled in one of those slightly sinful-looking bars which are prevalent in the upper Midwest, with very dim emerald-green lighting like the Tunnel of Fear at a fun fair, a décor which flits uneasily between Tahiti (rattan chairs and plastic orchids) and France (naughty murals in primary colours), and a staff of talkative, crew-cut teenagers earning money for their "further education."

The drama gentlemen were cordial and welcoming and conveyed the impression that they did not regard us either as pretentious interlopers or a threat to their livelihood. This was nice, because several of the drama teachers whom we met in other places were jealous and touchy and regarded our project as superfluous. We had been told by one professor that drama in his territory was entirely satisfactorily taken care of by the productions of his students: "Why, my production of **Paint Your Wagon** packed the gymnasium for three nights."

There was an interview with the governor in the State Capitol at St. Paul. The Capitol was exactly what one thinks an American state capitol should look like— a modest but expensive, and not too literal, imitation of the Capitol in Washington, with dome, discreetly veiled statues of very similar ladies labelled Agriculture, Music, Justice, Forestry and Mrs. Clarence Heidegger. Within, there was a handsome staircase, lots of rosewood panelling and some simply terrible oil paintings of, and possibly by, former governors. The Governor, who was then Mr. Orville Freeman, received us kindly and listened with apparent interest to the pitch, which was now getting rather too slick and well-marshalled. Did we, or did I only hope we should, have glasses of sherry to match the colour of the rosewood panelling?

It was sunny. Everything during these two extremely busy days and nights took place either in brilliant sunshine, or else at night, in brilliant starlight sparkling upon snow like a child's dream of an iced cake.

From Minneapolis to Cleveland. We had been invited to talk with the Board of the Cleveland Playhouse. We genuinely admired its aims and its achievement; the board members, in turn, were friendly and kind. But well before the end of our two-day stay it was apparent that, despite the best of mutual good will, a marriage was not likely to take place.

From Cleveland to Milwaukee. Here again we

encountered genuine good will. The University, the rep-
resentatives of very important business firms, a considerable group of private citizens, all professed themselves
eager to support such a scheme as we proposed. Clearly
we could reckon on Milwaukee as at least a strong
possibility.

From Milwaukee to Detroit. Here again the interest
was serious and strong; almost, we felt, too serious.
Executives of the automobile industry, rushing at seven
(P.M.) from their desks, which they reached at seven
(A.M.) five days a week for forty-eight weeks of the
year, glared with unsmiling intensity from behind thick
lenses while we made our pitch. Their questions, put
politely but with unsmiling intensity, showed that they
had listened to us with remarkable concentration. From
what we said they had extracted every ounce of factual
information; their questions were practical and interesting. Were we unjust, I wonder, to think that, as well as
extracting the facts, they had also extracted every
ounce of humour, of pleasure, of potential poetry and
discarded these impractical ingredients firmly and
forever?

But the interest was there and the practicality had
to be admired. A week or two after our visit we received an elaborate, immensely efficient dossier, setting
forth how money could be raised, by whom, by when
and how much. Of the programme or the policy there
was never a word. This may well have been because
they regarded the fund-raising as their business and the
rest as ours, and were delicately reluctant to interfere.

Dr. Sachar's had been a most generous offer; we
knew that at Brandeis we should have a wonderfully
bright and lively audience, but Brandeis is too near Boston. Boston is too much in the aura of Broadway; almost

every important Broadway production visits Boston
either just before, or just after, the New York run.

Our scheme, we felt, could only thrive if it were
right outside the Broadway orbit and only so could it be
really useful.

San Francisco never seemed to be a serious starter
as regards our project. The choice, therefore, lay between Detroit, Milwaukee and the Twin Cities.

It was now late in the fall of 1959. My wife and I
departed for Ireland, where I took ill and nearly died.

The crucial choice between our suitors had therefore to be made by Rea and Zeisler.

Early in the New Year (1960) they revisited Detroit,
Milwaukee and Minneapolis, saw again many of the
people whom we had seen before and talked with
them more specifically and in greater detail. They also
made new contacts and got new impressions.

As I began to recover, they were in close touch
with me. Almost daily letters were exchanged. But for
three months I was no more than a sleeping partner.
Decisions, they felt, must for better or for worse, be
taken by the end of May.

But we had certain misgivings.

Detroit was too large, too sprawling a community.
Our scheme, we felt, would not be sufficiently spectacular to make any kind of a splash in the already considerable programmes of culture and entertainment.
Better to be a bigger frog in a smaller pond.

Again, though we believed that in Detroit the fund-
raising would be more quickly and easily accomplished
than anywhere else, we were nervous of the Big Business interests. We had no rational grounds for the
suspicion, but we did suspect that those who pay the
larger proportion of the piper's fee would expect, how-

ever unmusical, to call the tune; and we did not feel confident of our power to refute this widely held but entirely unreasonable assumption.

In the Detroit area are several important universities, and several of lesser importance. Again we may have been quite unduly suspicious that our project might become a shuttlecock batted back and forth between rival institutions. The suspicion was unsupported by tangible evidence, there were merely **a priori** grounds for supposing that such a situation might arise. It could all too easily have arisen, for instance, in connection with the location of the project. We would have been reluctant to settle in downtown Detroit, which like the centre of so many other cities becomes a depressing, and even dangerous, desert after the shops and offices have shut. If we went to Ann Arbor, or Dearborn, or Grosse Pointe, we feared that other suburbs would regard us as being part of whatever community we happened to be in. They seemed so insular, spiritually so very far apart.

Milwaukee had much to commend it. We had been impressed by the people whom we had met there. We could draw on a large population locally, also it was part of a very populous and prosperous region and within easy range of Chicago. But, in fact, would that proximity to be a good or a bad thing? Chicago, like Detroit, is a huge complex of leisure activities. We might again be a small frog in a large and turbulent pond.

Finally, we realised that Milwaukee was already committed to a fund-raising campaign in aid of an Urban Renewal Project. I think it was proposed that this project be widened to include a theatre as well as a concert hall. But we felt that inevitably our comparatively small project would get swamped in a great number of other schemes and activities. Excellent and valuable as we were sure that these would be, we felt that they could not fail to be competitors, whose very excellence only made them more dangerous. Moreover, we were unable to discover just when the Urban Renewal Project would come into operation. The money required was tremendous, there were so many personalities, so many ideas involved, that we could not but foresee delay. Five years, or even ten, we feared, might elapse before we finally opened our doors.

We still inclined towards the Twin Cities. Of all our suitors they were the farthest removed from Broadway. It is true that the population, both of the cities themselves and of the surrounding area, was a good deal smaller than that of Milwaukee or Detroit. But the population, we thought, was large enough to support a theatre, and small enough to enable us to be a big frog.

We put considerable stock in the strong ties which seemed possible between ourselves and the university. It is already a vast institution, and envisages over the next ten years a colossal expansion. By 1970 an enrollment is expected of over 42,000 students.

It is, I guess, arguable whether such wholesaling provides the best educational results. There are many arguments for and against. What cannot be argued is that the alliance with, and good will of, such a Behemoth is an absolute necessity for all other cultural endeavours in the region.

We had been impressed and touched by the generous and unselfish attitude of Frank Whiting and his staff. We did not at this stage see precisely how we and they could be useful to one another; but we felt confident that we could, and that here—in the bridging of just one gap between a professional and an academic theatre—something of permanent value might be begun.

Finally, we put considerable stock in the good will and assistance of John Cowles, Jr., and others whom we had met in Minneapolis and St. Paul.

Meantime the weeks were passing, the deadline was approaching, but out of Minnesota there came no sign. Let us "cut," as in a movie, from Rea and Zeisler in New York, scanning with dwindling hopes the horizon for smoke signals from the Northwest, to Cowles and his associates in Minnesota.

As the year 1959 was ending, a so-called Steering Committee had been formed to guide the incipient project. This committee consisted of John Cowles, Jr., of the "Minneapolis Star and Tribune"; Otto Silha and Philip Von Blon, also on the staff of the newspaper; Louis Zelle, president of the Jefferson Bus Company; Frank Whiting, director of the University Theatre; Roger Kennedy, vice-president of the Northwestern National Bank of St. Paul; Pierce Butler III, a lawyer from St. Paul; Justin Smith of the T. B. Walker Foundation, and Harvard Arnason, then curator of the Walker Art Center, later transferred to the Guggenheim Museum in New York.

These represented a responsible and influential section of society in the Twin Cities. Some, not all of them, were wealthy, but none of them needed this project for his own advancement, either socially or financially. Demonstrably they were giving their services for the benefit of the community.

They are a youngish group, most of them well under fifty, some under forty. I suppose that it would be right to assume that they are not exactly the community's top-brass, who would be men in their sixties and seventies; but they are, perhaps, a generation of Heirs Apparent.

But absolutely these men do not form a compact little group of rich and powerful people. It is a highly diverse group, in background, wealth, religion, race and attitude. Only by being so, I think, were these men able to catch the public imagination and to plant the project firmly in the locality.

It is still too early to know whether, in fact, our theatre is firmly rooted. But if it is, and if eventually it brings forth good fruit, it will be to this first, dedicated and extremely diverse group that thanks are due.

They met weekly, and first began to investigate the possibilities of remodelling existing theatres in the Twin Cities. Rather soon they decided that this idea was unlikely to be fruitful. They then started to work on plans for building a new theatre on the campus of the University of Minnesota. But this hare didn't run far either. For some reason, the business community did not seem enthusiastic about giving money for a project on the campus.

Early in the spring of 1960 John Cowles, Jr., made a proposal to the Annual Meeting of the Board of the T. B. Walker Foundation. The Foundation had been considering building an auditorium to hold some of the activities which, in addition to the Art Gallery, it sponsors—concerts, lectures, performances by dance groups, chamber opera.

Cowles' proposal was that the board should donate land behind the Walker Art Center and, in addition, make some contribution to the theatre project which he and his associates were sponsoring. In return the Foundation should share the use of the building.

The site is central, yet it is quiet. It faces a green lawn and a formal flower garden, handsomely maintained by the City of Minneapolis.

The Walker Foundation agreed to give this beautiful and suitable site and, in addition, pledged a tiny cash contribution of four hundred thousand dollars.

In May, 1960, no more than a week before the agreed Day of Decision, a wire was received by Rea and Zeisler, who had, more or less, written off Minnesota and were wondering whether to send a corsage, candy and a sapphire ring to Milwaukee or to Detroit. Would they meet the Minneapolis steering committee for luncheon in New York?

The private plane of the "Minneapolis Star and Tribune" brought the steering committee to the luncheon. Over the salmon mayonnaise many questions were batted back and forth about both the practical details of the project and its philosophical implications.

Over coffee, Cowles, as spokesman for the Steering Committee, said that they liked the project, would do their utmost to implement it, had the promise of what they considered a suitable site, to say nothing of four hundred thousand dollars. He believed that they could raise another nine hundred thousand, making a total of one million and three hundred thousand dollars.

Rea and Zeisler, the artistic, dreamy things, heads in the clouds, said, "If it takes more, do you think you can raise more?"

Cowles, the ice-cold, iron Man of Affairs, said "Yes."

There was no promise. No documents were signed. No hyperbolical expressions were uttered of enthusiasm or confidence. But then I do not think anyone could describe John Cowles, Jr., as a hyperbolical type. Enthusiasm was implicit in their having come to New York. Confidence was mutual.

Sweating heavily, trembling at the knees, our two Parises proffered the golden apple to Aphrodite, quite effectively disguised as a Steering Committee from the Upper Midwest.

I have suggested the reasons why we wanted the Twin Cities to support us. But reasons, I seem to have found out, are nearly always invented **after** a decision to defend, even excuse it. Inclinations, hunches have far more to do with crucial decisions than has reason.

We offered our rather runty little apple mostly because we **wanted** to work in the Twin Cities. Why? The weather? The people? The river? We have discussed it often and we simply do not know.

At this stage all we could say was: "If you want us, we're available. We will put our various skills, experiences at your service. We will create for you a professional theatre, which you will own. We shall be no more than paid hands. If we are unsatisfactory, you can, but not till after three years, get rid of us. You, however, must undertake the formidable task of raising the dough."

During that summer (1960) the steering committee was formally constituted on a non-profit basis as the Tyrone Guthrie Theatre Foundation. Louis Gelfand was appointed as Administrator, an office was loaned by the Walker Foundation in the Jade and Pottery Gallery. Never was a budding theatrical enterprize more elegantly, more splendidly housed.

Professor Ralph Rapson was now engaged to prepare plans for the building. Trained at the Massachusetts Institute of Technology, he had been for some

years Professor of Architecture at the University of
Minnesota and had, in addition to academic distinction,
a very varied and considerable practical record.

Now the task of fund-raising was begun in earnest.
Four hundred thousand dollars had been pledged. The
target was estimated at thirteen hundred thousand.
Nine hundred thousand therefore remained to be
found.

A finance committee was formed under the chair-
manship of Louis Zelle. Its members undertook the
arduous chore of personally soliciting contributions both
from firms and from well-off individuals. In addition,
scores of speeches were made to Groups.

I do not know how all the others managed. I
found it very hard work indeed. For no more than ten
days that summer Oliver Rea and I joined the evangeli-
cal campaign. Kind hostesses would invite us and a
group of their friends to lunch. Over the coffee we
would Make Our Pitch. In the evening, masculine organ-
izations—clubs, church groups, business associations—
would give us dinner. Over the coffee we would Make
Our Pitch. In between we would visit schools, talk on
the radio, make winsome, but progressively more
jaded, appearances on TV. After only ten days, neither
of us ever wished to look a martini in the face again
and had difficulty not making compulsive recruiting
speeches to one another in the men's room or as we
sped by taxi from one engagement to the next.

In October the architect's plans were submitted for
bids from contractors. The very lowest bid exceeded
the committee's expectation by several hundred thousand dollars. This was charming. The committee had no
option but to instruct the architect to revise his plans.
But even considerable revision did not relieve the neces-

sity of raising the target for the fund drive. The finance
committee, panting already and lolling its collective
tongue, was informed that a further seven hundred
thousand dollars would be required.

The Walker Foundation proffered a further hundred thousand over and above its already generous
contribution. The rest was dredged up somehow, although not without difficulty, and thanks to the energy
and splendid pertinacity of the committee and to the
generosity of the community the necessary sum eventually was reached. Contributions came from nearly three
thousand sources, from corporations, foundations, professional men, businessmen, from clubs and schools,
even from things called Women. The largest contribution was from the T. B. Walker Foundation, the smallest
from a Sunday-school class in Mankato, a small Minnesota town some eighty miles southwest of Minneapolis.
The class raised six dollars and thirty-seven cents.

Meantime, talking of Women, Gelfand had recruited a group of thirty or forty lady-volunteers who,
during this period, typed correspondence, worked a
duplicating machine, stuffed and stamped envelopes,
telephoned, filed and generally acted as unpaid but
indispensable office workers.

In June 1962 it was suggested to one of these
ladies, Mrs. Robert Wohlrabe, that she undertake to
expand this group and organise it on a more official
basis. She agreed, and under her presidency about two
hundred women formed themselves into a society called
the Stagehands. In addition to arranging a roster of
office work, the Stagehands spent many hours in the
preparation of a mailing list for the first ticket campaign.

By the end of 1962 the society expanded to a

total of twelve hundred women, in preparation for a drive to sell season tickets. Members were recruited from towns all over Minnesota, and were organized into areas, each with its own chairman and officers.

On January 20, 1963, a meeting was held in the still uncompleted theatre. In a temperature seventeen degrees below zero, more than seven hundred women assembled and sat themselves down on the cold concrete, listened to a rousing blast on the Horn of Roland delivered by Robert Preston, looked at Rita Gam and received, from their own officers, their final eve-of-battle instructions. They then went into action. Armed with literature and a disc upon which had been recorded not only Preston's Horn of Roland speech, but others by Hume Cronyn, Douglas Campbell and various persons about to be connected with the project, they launched themselves upon their various communities.

The ladies did not actually sell tickets. They sold the idea, glowed to friends and neighbors about the project, answered questions, urged people to order tickets and told them how to do so. It is computed that in the following eight weeks more than eight hundred coffee parties were held. One couple gave a dinner party for eight other couples and raffled a season ticket. Then they urged the other eight couples to go and do likewise. More than forty different dinner parties can be traced to that particular effort.

A Speaker's Bureau was organized, evangelists—thirty to forty men and women—were briefed and more than two hundred speeches were made to clubs, church groups and so on.

The campaign closed on March 25, 1963. Almost twenty-two thousand people had bought season tickets, giving them admission to each of the four productions. That is to say eighty-eight thousand seats had been sold for a total of rather more than two hundred seventy thousand dollars—a very substantial result indeed.

Throughout the year a nucleus of two hundred Stagehands continued to work for the theatre, as office help, assisting the actors to find housing and doing all sorts of useful but inconspicuous bits and pieces.

At the end of 1963 the organization was again expanded to something like twelve hundred, in preparation for the second season's ticket campaign.

All this has been of immense assistance to the business side of the enterprise. But I think it has more significance than that. These women gave a great deal of their time and energy, and sustained their effort over a considerable period. This would not have happened if they had just been stage-struck. Quite evidently they had the Cause not only at heart but in mind. They wanted the community to have a theatre of some quality and they were determined that it should not fail for lack of public support.

In fact, we have been able to offer them very little reward—no money, no glamour, really nothing but the feeling that the whole venture is in some part their own creation.

The Stagehands are perhaps the most conspicuous, but by no means the only instance of the solid support which the community has offered to this project. One of the members of the theatre staff, Minnesota born and raised and therefore far better placed than I to know about all this, has written as follows: "I feel very strongly that one of the primary reasons we were successful at the box office in the very first year of operation was because of the number of people in the

Midwest in high schools, colleges, community theatres and stock companies who had been working very hard for years to interest people in the living theatre. All of these people had 'prepared' an audience for us.

"And then Don Stoltz has been working for years with his Equity Company at the Old Log Theatre, refusing to give up, and continually trying to interest new people in theatre. I am sure that through his efforts over the past nineteen years he has given us several thousand people who would not otherwise have been ready to accept and welcome what we offer."

I am convinced that this is true. I would estimate that less than half of those who saw our **Hamlet** had ever seen a professional production of a Shakespeare play; and less than a quarter of those who saw **The Three Sisters** had ever seen a professional production of Chekhov. Nevertheless it was apparent that they were "prepared."

And as to Mr. Stoltz, where he might have been jealous and bitter that newcomers were established in a handsome playhouse considerably larger than his own and that our project was able to attract more public attention and more funds than his, he was generous and helpful. And where he might have feared that our arrival would damage his business, he was confident that we should assist one another. I am happy to say that his confidence has, so far, been entirely justified. Last season, when we were both in operation and both therefore competing for the same trade, his theatre did better business than in any previous summer of its history.

Hamlet

Opened May 7, 1963. Designed by Tanya Moiseiwitsch.
With George Grizzard as Hamlet, Jessica Tandy as
the Queen, Lee Richardson as Claudius, Robert Pastene
as Polonius, Ellen Geer as Ophelia.

Three Sisters

Opened June 18, 1963. Designed by Tanya Moiseiwitsch.
With Jessica Tandy as Olga, Rita Gam as Masha,
Ellen Geer as Irina.

5

Architect and Client

The committee, an enlargement of the same group who had flown to New York, now divided itself into several parts. There was a fund-raising committee and a building committee. The latter now commissioned Ralph Rapson, Professor of Architecture at the University of Minnesota, to design the theatre.

In what follows, I shall write frankly of our relations with Professor Rapson, which were not wholly satisfactory to either party. A certain amount of friction and mutual misunderstanding must, I guess, be inevitable in a project which demands the co-operation between an architect and a group of clients who consider that they have expert views about the function of the building, based on a professional experience which the architect does not share.

My sole object in even alluding to disagreement is to indicate and illustrate some of the great difficulties inherent in the relation between architect and client, particularly when a public building is in queston; further, the relation between patron (our building committee) and architect (Rapson); and between architect (Rapson) and fellow-artists (Tanya Moiseiwitsch, Douglas Campbell and myself), engaged upon different aspects of the same project. Analogous difficulties are bound to confront any group of people which embarks upon a project similar to this one of ours in the Twin

Cities. It is to such people that I assume this book may be of interest; and it can be more useful to them if I discuss our difficulties frankly.

Our first big decision was whether the theatre should be built with a proscenium dividing stage from auditorium by means of an arch with a curtain, which when lowered would conceal the stage from the spectators, and when raised would reveal a picture. Or, alternatively, whether the stage should jut out into an auditorium, which should sweep around it to form an arc of about one hundred eighty degrees. Or—yet another alternative—whether we should try to achieve a building which should somehow be convertible from open stage to proscenium and vice versa.

Rapson felt confident that he could achieve a convertible theatre. But we felt no less confident that the result must be a compromise, in which neither proscenium nor open stage would be fully realised. He acquiesced and it was agreed that we would not even attempt to be "convertible."

I shall not embark upon a lengthy consideration of the respective advantages and disadvantages of the proscenium and open stage. The matter has been frequently debated elsewhere and the arguments are easily accessible.

It was clear that the proscenium had the advantage of being the more usual way to build a theatre; it was what most people regarded as the right way to build a stage; more importantly, it was the sort of stage for which practically all plays had been written since the middle of the seventeenth century.

On the other hand, plays written before the middle of the seventeenth century had been written for open stages; and a rather impressive number of important

plays were written before the middle of the seventeenth
century. A classical repertory clearly would have to
lean quite heavily upon both the Greeks and the Eliza-
bethans. Moreover, it was our belief, though at this
juncture this could not be proved, that an open stage
could be considerably more flexible than might appear
to the lay mind. Further, more people can be got into
the same amount of cubic space if they are seated
around an open stage, rather than **facing** a proscenium.
Preliminary budgets had shown us that, if the theatre
were to achieve the sort of standard at which we were
aiming, it could only pay its way if the capacity were
around fifteen hundred persons. Fifteen hundred cannot
be intimately accommodated in a proscenium theatre.
But when folded around an open stage none of them
need sit further away than the fourteenth row, approxi-
mately fifty feet from the middle of the stage. If you
are going to offer the sort of programme which demands the serious concentration of the audience, then
it is essential that actor and audience be brought into
the closest possible mutual contact.

But to my mind even more important is the fact
that the proscenium stage is deliberately designed to
encourage the audience to believe that events on stage
are "really" taking place, to accept a palpable fiction
for fact; whereas the open stage discourages "illusion"
and emphasizes that a play is a ritual in which the audience is invited to participate. The audience is so
arranged that spectators can see one another around,
and beyond, the more brightly lighted stage. This certainly does not encourage illusion. You can hardly be
expected to believe that you are right there at the
Court of King Arthur when just over Lancelot's left ear
you can descry, dim but unmistakable, the Halversons,

who keep the corner store. This, however, does emphatically, and I think valuably, imply that theatre-going is a sociable, a shared experience, and that the audience, unlike the audience for movies or television, has an active part to play, has to do its share towards creating the performance, can make or mar the occasion.

Finally, apart from these technical or philosophical considerations, we believed it would be a good idea to have an open stage simply because it was not the obvious, conventional kind. It would stress, we felt, the experimental and pioneering character of the whole venture; it would be more of a talking-point; and, by providing a more three-dimensional entertainment, would emphasize the contrast between the live theatre and movies or TV. This contrast is less marked when a play is framed by a rectangular proscenium, like the rectangular movie or TV screen.

We discussed with Ralph Rapson the desirability of making an audience feel that it is a unity; and that this is largely brought about by not allowing those in the cheaper or less fashionable seats to feel that they are only second-class citizens. He came up with three of four suggested designs for the auditorium. All were interesting. One we particularly liked, and so did he; so the choice was easy.

The second-class-citizen problem was ingeniously solved by blurring the division between upstairs and down, between orchestra and balcony. One whole section of the auditorium, nearly a third of the whole, is designed to rise from floor level to the level of the back of the balcony in one unbroken slope. The back five or six rows of this section then sweep round the remaining two-thirds of the auditorium as a balcony. The device makes the whole auditorium asymmetrical, an effect which is further stressed by the asymmetrical shape of the stage—an extremely irregular pentagon—and by the fact that it does not jut out into the auditorium at a radial angle, but slightly askew. This asymmetricality had, we all believed, the effect of making the design more lively without being restless or undignified; also of making the building look even less like a traditional opera house or a movie theatre.

When I saw the plans I wanted the design of the auditorium to be modified in two respects: that the entire auditorium should be a little smaller, and that the balcony should be deeper, so that its front should more closely overhang the stage. Both these suggestions were based on lessons learned at Stratford, Ontario, where in my opinion the house is just a little bit too large and the balcony too remote from the stage. Rapson agreed to reduce the diameter of the semi-circular auditorium, cutting off one, maybe two, rows at the back. The loss of capacity was considerable; the number of seats had to be reduced from nearly eighteen hundred to fourteen hundred and thirty-seven. But we all agreed that the gain in intimacy justified the loss. It has to be borne in mind that on an open-stage an actor cannot face every member of his auditory all the time. This creates not only a visual problem but also one of audibility. An open-stage demands that the back row of seats be close enough for all its occupants to hear actors who are speaking, even if only momentarily, with their backs turned to some of their auditors; also to make the actors clearly and expressively visible, so that when one speaker's face is turned away the face and reaction of his interlocutor may help the audience to get the message.

My second suggestion, that the balcony be deepened so that its front would be closer to the stage, was rejected. Rapson felt that if this were done, the front of the balcony, though it would not actually obstruct the sight line of those underneath, in the back of the orchestra, would overhang them in a rather claustrophobic way and would make it hard for them to hear. Now that the theatre is built, I am inclined to think that in this matter we were needlessly cautious. But, at the discussion stage, when the only available evidence is a plan on a very reduced scale (¼ inch = 1 foot), it is very hard to visualise the essential dimensions and proportions; consequently it is all too easy to lose confidence in your own opinion.

My insistence upon trying to have as little empty cubic space as possible in the auditorium, and my belief that comfort is less important than intimacy, that only when its members are jammed together does an audience generate the right kind of heat and excitement, may, I now think, have distressed Rapson. These ideas were quite uncongenial to him.

Moreover, our group had now been joined by Tanya Moiseiwitsch and Douglas Campbell. We three had been colleagues for a long time. Miss Moiseiwitsch had designed the stage at Stratford, Ontario, ten years before, and it had been the outcome of long discussion and much experiment for years even before that. Campbell had been playing leading parts at Stratford for ten years and had directed several productions there. We made, perhaps, a rather formidably compact alliance and I now see that we tried to clinch too many arguments by saying, "Well, at Stratford we learned . . . at Stratford we always . . ." and, most annoying of all, "At Stratford we never . . ."

In a sense we were right. Stratford, Ontario, had

established technical precedent. We were in possession of valuable, indeed unique, professional knowledge. But no doubt we could have been more tactful in the way we trotted it out. Also, looking back, I can imagine that, partly just by being three against one, we seemed to be pushing Ralph Rapson's back against a wall.

The situation was not eased by a trip to Stratford, once more in the "Tribune's" private plane, by a delegation of our committee accompanied by Professor Rapson. He was not favourably impressed. Neither the exterior nor the interior of the Stratford Theatre pleased him at all. He was interested in neither the acting nor the productions. He found the experience claustrophobic —"All those **people** all **around** me."

We felt somewhat chastened. We wondered whether our enthusiasm had been excessive, whether we viewed our dear Stratford through glasses rose-tinted by sentimentality and egotism. I suppose we may perhaps have been rather tactless and boring, but we felt that Stratford provided the only available reference to so many technical points which we considered important.

Meantime, all was not going well between Ralph Rapson and those who were responsible for the technical equipment of the theatre. Peter Zeisler is an extremely experienced theatre technician, and, to reinforce him in the special field of stage-lighting, the board had engaged Jean Rosenthal, a world authority on this topic. From an architect's point of view, perhaps their ideas seemed impractical or odd. In any case, Rapson did not seem favourably impressed. The situation was not assisted by the fact that while he was in the Twin Cities they were, except for flying visits, in New York.

The next crisis arose over the design of the stage-set. This was the province of Tanya Moiseiwitsch. She, Douglas Campbell and I were of the opinion that a permanent and architectural construction such as she had designed for Stratford Ontario, would not be satisfactory. There the stage is intended primarily, if not exclusively, for plays of Shakespeare. The theatre in the Twin Cities must attempt to cope with a more varied repertoire, must aim to be more flexible.

The design eventually agreed between us was of two immense sliding doors or screens, which, when closed, formed a sort of corrugated wall. They were on wheels and could slide apart, but not to disclose a picture. Such a picture would not be visible to more than the central section of the audience; and, anyway, it was entirely contrary to our philosophy to push aside doors—equivalent to a curtain—and disclose A Picture. The doors would open merely to permit wagons, previously set with furniture and properties as required, to be pushed out onto the stage.

The doors were pierced with apertures both at floor level and at second-floor window or balcony height. These apertures could be closed with cabinet-made, precisely fitted panels, or else could be opened to represent windows or doors. A balcony could be placed so as to be accessible from the upstairs apertures. Many small but significant variations were possible.

In due course, this design was shown to Rapson. Miss Moiseiwitsch was anxious that her work should harmonise with his. He looked at the model in silence, then expressed the view that it had neither character nor style. What modifications would he care to propose? Was it possible that "character" was not perhaps the best idea in a permanent set, which would be seen in every production and must therefore be flexible and must, of all things, not be obtrusive? The discussion then began to revolve around matters of proportion and the relation of various elements to the whole. About all this Rapson's views were interesting. We, of course, preferred our own. At length, the meeting was adjourned till the following morning. No conclusions had been reached. Miss Moiseiwitsch, who had worked for several months on the model, was tense but firm. The rest of us were very tense indeed.

Next morning Rapson brought us a roll of tracing paper, on which overnight he had produced his own design for the set. I regret to say that a scene ensued. The meeting broke up, like the disastrous theatricals at Elsinore, in most admired disorder. The episode was never referred to again. The Moiseiwitsch design was used and, for our purposes, worked excellently.

There were two more crises: the first, when it emerged that the cost of the building was going considerably to exceed the estimates. This was no one's fault. Between the time of estimate and the actual building, months had elapsed during which prices of materials and services had risen. In a rather large project like this every single possible expense, delay and error simply cannot be foreseen. Probably the budget should have allowed a higher figure for contingencies, but none of us thought of this until too late.

A serious error, however, was now made by the Building Committee and ourselves, in agreeing to an unbalanced scheme of retrenchment. In outline this involved a reduction of about twenty feet in the length of the building, the entire reduction to be made backstage. We did query this, suggesting that the foyers and front-of-house arrangements, which seemed to be handsomely but needlessly spacious, might at least share the cut in space.

Rapson opposed this suggestion for a number of reasons, which were highly technical. But what greatly influenced the committee's agreement was that we were told that if we did not agree, the building could not be ready in time, and the opening, which by now had been announced for the spring of 1963, would have to be postponed for a year.

The reduction of space backstage involved grave loss of amenities. Originally many of the workrooms and offices gave onto the open air. But now it became necessary to place a passage along the outside wall, and workrooms and offices became prison cells totally removed from daylight, windowless, airless except for a sort of hot wind, a sirocco, which came roaring out of something called a Duct.

The people who work in this part of the building have, during the season, to be in the theatre from early in the morning until late in the evening; whereas the foyers are used for only a few brief minutes at the beginning and end of performances and during the intermissions. It is true that spacious and handsome foyers make a pleasant impression and add to the theatre's prestige, while no one except the workers involved knows about backstage arrangements. The pass door in our theatre is rather like a bulkhead separating first-class accommodation from steerage; carpeted elegance gives place abruptly to cheerless accommodation for the Lower Orders.

All of us agreed to this decision, but I now believe it was wrong. We should have insisted upon the reduction of space being more equitably divided between front and backstage, refused to accept less than adequate workrooms and offices, and risked the consequences.

In November 1961, at eight of a bitterly cold morning, the committee, the architect and his staff, Oliver Rea, Peter Zeisler, Tanya Moiseiwitsch, Douglas Campbell and myself, the office staff, a group of newspaper, radio and television reporters and technicians, together with sundry friends and wellwishers, assembled for the ceremony of Turning the First Sod.

To me was accorded the honour of performing this symbolic act. My tiny hand was frozen, and into it someone thrust a coal shovel. I had hoped, naturally, for a gold and platinum trowel with a moving inscription on its mother-of-pearl handle. But in the flurry of events this had been overlooked and at the eleventh hour someone had produced the shovel from the furnace room of the Walker Art Center.

I was very grateful, because otherwise I should have had to Turn the Sod, which was frozen harder than steel, with my bare hands. It was apparent that to turn even an eggspoonful of earth would require a superhuman effort. At the first attempt the shovel buckled pitifully. There was a faint titter. I bent it back ino shape and tried again. After several attempts, red in the face and grunting heavily, I had turned enough earth to bury a flea. An anonymous lady—I shall love her for it always—scooped together the six or seven grains and declared that she would plant an acorn in them.

At this moment from behind our backs a giant bulldozer appeared. With a roar it pushed over a nice butternut tree, which fell in a tangle of smashed branches and severed roots. Must we always advance into new territory over dead bodies?

Someone shouted "Coffee!" Thankful to get out of the sub-zero wind, we all fled into the bowels of the Walker Art Center. Outside we could hear the growls and snarls of a power saw, dismembering the carcass of the butternut. In what I could not help thinking was rather a furtive way the assistant janitor of Walker was poking something into the furnace. It was the broken handle of my shovel.

Our final difficulty over the building occurred early in the spring of 1962. It was concerned with the exterior. The plans and elevations gave no clue as to what it would eventually look like. The members of the Building Committee, reasonably enough, felt that they would like to know. Rapson explained, also reasonably, that to Render plans and elevations, so as to give a fair impression of the final result was a highly specialised matter. He himself did not profess to be able to do it, nor did he think that anyone in the Twin Cities was adequately qualified. A firm in Los Angeles was ultimately commissioned. Their charges struck the committee as rather high, but there seemed no alternative but to cough up.

After a delay of many weeks the Rendering appeared. It was a thoroughly vulgar and flashy piece of work. In front of some "stylized" trees, some "stylized" Hollywoody ladies were strolling; some "stylized," very brightly coloured automobiles were depicted; and behind all this, well in the background, was a representation—also "stylized"—of an entirely undistinguished, rectangular structure, plastered with posters bearing

elegant legends like **"Hamlet** tonite." From the structure's flat roof ascended a line of flagpoles bearing
bright-coloured pennants. They gave it the air of syn-
thetic gaiety aimed at by used-car lots and cut-rate
shopping centres.

This work of art received from the building committee a rather chilly response. The delay had been inconvenient and alarming; and the committee, having
been already compelled to one unsatisfactory decision
under threat of postponement, was determined not to
be so stampeded again. The fee to Los Angeles, which
had always seemed large, seemed now completely outrageous.

Rapson agreed that the Rendering had not come
up to expectation and that it did not quite represent his
conception. He appreciated the committee's desire to
know what its building was going to look like, and
thought that the best plan now would be for himself
and staff to make a model.

"Thank you," said the chairman. "We should be
glad to see it tomorrow."

And on the morrow, to Ralph's great credit, a
model was ready. He and his staff were pale, they had
dark circles under their eyes, they yawned a good deal.
A child of nine could have inferred an all-night sitting.

The exterior as shown on this model was interesting and, except for a certain rectangularity, bore not
the least resemblance to the dreadful Rendering. The
chairman, I think, repented a little of his previous
severity. The reaction was general. Everyone admired
the gameness which had produced an elaborate model
at almost magical speed. Everyone now **wanted** to like
the design; everyone now **did** like the design.

The model showed the elliptical auditorium sitting

inside a glass box; round the glass box was an open-work structure which resembled a basket made, so it turned out, of plywood covered with Granolex.

I and, I think, the rest of the committee failed to appreciate one or two very relevant points. The open-work structure does not, as I had supposed, take any share in the support of the building. It is solely ornamental.

Moreover, the glass box, though it looks well, is neither cheap nor practical, since it requires plenty of maintenance.

In any event, I think that the committee ought not to have agreed to so costly an exterior, however good-looking, since it was achieved by drastic economies backstage. I do not question Professor Rapson's taste. It does not fully accord with my own, but in architecture his is the expert, professional point of view. I do, however, question the philosophy which in several instances put handsome appearance ahead of function and the comfort and convenience of those who are to work in the building.

But let me close this chapter, as it began, with the admission that there are two sides to every question. While we have not always seen eye to eye with Professor Rapson on this project, we still know him to be a very able and versatile architect. Furthermore, we agree that, despite certain reservations, there is a great deal to admire about the building.

And I guess that in the entire history of mankind few important buildings have ever been put up about which the owners, or occupiers or lessees have not had certain reservations.

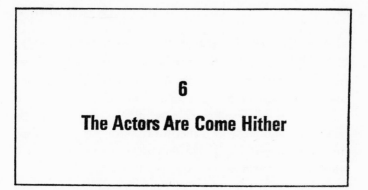

6

The Actors Are Come Hither

In January, 1962, we began to recruit the company of actors, and to choose the programme of plays.

You might think that one of the two processes should precede the other; that either you pick the plays and then look for actors who suit the parts; or, alternatively, you find three or four leading actors and then choose plays to suit them. In fact the two processes—and this I have learnt through an experience of many years and many repertory companies—must be achieved simultaneously, and cannot be achieved fast.

In this case we began with two leading players. Hume Cronyn and Jessica Tandy offered their services for the season. Both are extremely talented, versatile and experienced players. The plan was that each of them would play in three out of a repertoire of four plays, which would be chosen to offer a bold contrast in dramatic styles. Therefore versatility was essential. Moreover their names are well known; they would offer both to our audience and, not less importantly, to other actors a certain reassurance that standards were likely to be high, that we were not just a small, well-intentioned but slightly amateurish venture in the wilderness. Finally, we all knew the Cronyns well enough to count on them as responsible leaders of the company.

This is important. On Broadway it is inconvenient, but not disastrous, if stars behave foolishly or irrespon-

sibly. But we well knew that, if our venture were to succeed, the morale of the company must be high. They
were going to have to see a very great deal of one
another, often in anxious and tiring circumstances; a
high degree of unselfish co-operation was going to be
needed. The morale of a theatre company is established
and maintained by its leading actors; they are, as it
were, at the head of the troops in the field.

Therefore we accepted the offer of the Cronyns'
services with delight. It was agreed that each of them
should play one leading part, one good and one supporting part, and have one play "out." We explained
that the repertoire was not yet chosen, but that we
hoped in a few weeks to discuss specific plays and parts.
The first step had been taken.

This commitment helpfully limited and defined our
field of choice. It seemed a sensible plan—I am still not
sure whether it really was so—to open with a big production of an important Shakespeare play—**Hamlet,**
maybe, if we could find a suitable American actor for
the leading part. Prominent on the agenda from now
on was the search for an interesting young actor to
play Hamlet.

We began to hold auditions in the summer.
Literally hundreds of actors and actresses applied,
amongst them many whose names are well known.
Clearly it was not going to be quite so difficult, as some
of our more pessimistic friends had warned us, to
persuade people to leave the bright lights of Broadway
and lucrative possibilities of television for quite a pro-
longed sojourn in the upper Midwest. The prospect of
three parts in quick succession and in important plays
was evidently a strong attraction.

The mechanics of the Audition are extremely unsatisfactory. However considerate and courteous the management tries to be, it is still an ordeal, and sometimes a degrading ordeal, for the actor. He has to step out alone upon the stage and in the course of three or four minutes must convince three or four strangers, sitting out front in the darkness, that they wish to employ him. All too often the employers know nothing about the art or craft of acting, and are completely insensitive about the actor's feelings. They just know that they are looking for someone to play a Moneylender or the Manageress of a Laundry, in which case they look for the Type, whatever that may be. "Not quite the Type, dear," they say to those who are not going to get the job. More often they are just looking for something sexually attractive. And again the stock phrase of rejection is: "Not quite the Type, dear, just not **quite** the Type."

In our case we were not, at this stage, looking for any particular Types. Of course, it never does any harm if actors or actresses are handsome and sexually alluring. But, in His Almighty Wisdom, God has not always arranged that the handsomest and sexiest of His creatures shall be the most talented, or even at all intelligent.

A classical repertoire demands talent and demands intelligence. Beauty and sex appeal can to a great extent be achieved by artifice. What cannot be faked is vocal quality.

Oddly, this is the part of their equipment to which the American actors pay only the most perfunctory attention. Personality, today's great euphemism for sex appeal, they cultivate with studious, even fanatical, zeal. But few of them seem ever to have thought about what, if anything, distinguishes "good" speech from "bad."

It has not occurred to them that a great rhetorical speech is an aria, which demands great technical accomplishment; careful shaping, so that climax and anti-climax are arranged to assist and not confuse the meaning of the passage; phrasing as conscious, and breathing as controlled, as that of a singer; awareness of rhythm; precise judgment of stresses, pauses, tempi; conscious use of legato and staccato and rubato . . . if you use these Italian musical terms to most American actors, they either laugh heartily because they think it is madly funny to talk Foreign, or else they write you off with silent contempt as a long-haired, decadent nut. Most of them simply have not the faintest idea of how to analyse a piece of rhetoric and then how to translate that analysis into practical vocal terms.

It must be remembered that in current American life it is considered not only unimportant but unacceptable to speak "well." It is thought to be un-American, undemocratic and unmanly. We shall return to this topic later.

Since we knew that at least two of our four plays would make considerable vocal demands, and that the other two could not but be helped by actors who had some vocal technique, this was what we sought above all else in the Auditions.

But again the inadequacy of the Audition smote us in the eye. Nervousness upsets everyone's vocal mechanism; your muscles are tense; your diaphragm is quivery, not firm; your throat is dry; you strain and press. Also, unfortunate accidents occur; eight people will, quite without premeditation, select the same piece. No one can blame managers who are also, though with less reason, nervous if, at the moment just before lunch when everyone is rumbling with hunger and has a headache from trying to concentrate, they are apt to under-

prise the eighth aspirant who comes on and begins "The quality of mercy is not strained."

ADVICE TO AUDITION CANDIDATES (free)

What follows is not intended for most readers, who are hereby warned to skip to the next section. But let me, out of a long experience, offer a few sentences of advice to those who may have to undergo the ordeal of an audition.

Choose several, or anyway two, strongly contrasted pieces; grave and gay, loud and soft, fast and slow, prose and verse. It does not matter, so long as they show that your lute has more than one string.

If you want to be heard in two pieces, each of them must be very short and should be chosen so that you can make some sort of impact in the first ten seconds. Ask at the beginning of your audition to be allowed to do **both** pieces; but take the curse off this request by explaining how short they are.

Do not choose the piece in which you were "coached" by an elocution teacher. Ten to one half the applicants have chosen to ride the very same warhorse. Also, do not choose some side-splitting comedy routine. It is apt to fall rather flat if there isn't a full house out front splitting its sides.

Stand still.

Act as though you believe your auditors may possibly be human beings, not witless and cruel ogres. Many actors seem unable to find a middle course between the obsequious and the impudent. All that is asked for is the good manners which you have a right to expect, but do not always get, from management.

Good manners, incidentally, also extend to your appearance. It is not good manners to apply for a job with dirty shoes, with dirty, unbrushed hair and generally looking as if you had just emerged from cleaning the sewers. Of course one in a thousand **may** be filling unwanted leisure and earning much-wanted money as a sewer cleaner. More power to your elbow; but the facts of the case should be summarized in order to explain your appearance. The other nine hundred and ninety-nine should pay a potential employer the compliment of assuming that he has enough sense not to confuse a beatnik appearance with talent, and enough sense to know that people who give auditions looking like slobs are remarkably likely to be slobs.

We tried to conduct our auditions in two stages. First an interview, in which we tried to get the applicant to talk a bit, partly to break the ice, partly to find out, even in the smallest degree, what lay behind the façade. Those who survived this ordeal were asked to give an audition on a stage, in a theatre, so that we could form some opinion about their power of projection.

In New York City, even in summer, it is not always possible to get the use of a suitable theatre. One lady gave her audition in competition with an electric drill which was actually poking a hole in the side of the building where we were, and which rendered nine out of ten words quite inaudible. The wall, her concentration and ours were all simultaneously and completely shattered. She behaved with exemplary patience and good manners. Had we had even remotely suitable parts for her, she would have been offered a second chance.

The first stage of these auditions gave us useful

information about what people had already done. It was possible to distinguish those who had gone out in search of the kind of parts—in the kind of plays—which we were planning to do, from those who had stuck around New York in pursuit of higher wages and quicker possibilities of "success." It also emerged, though we knew this already, how very few opportunities there are for young Americans to get the kind of experience which an artistically ambitious actor simply cannot forego. Practically all those whom we considered seriously had been either with the Cleveland Playhouse, the Washington Arena, the group called A.P.A.; or productions of Shakespeare in Central Park.

We saw several potential Hamlets; and, had we so desired, could have seen several dozens, even several hundreds. I was to direct **Hamlet,** but in the matter of choice I was in close consultation with Douglas Campbell, who was joining the company as assistant artistic director and was going to direct two of our four plays. At this time he was in New York, "co-starring" with Fredric March in Chayevsky's **Gideon.**

We agreed that we would prefer a Hamlet who was not too obviously "sensitive" (in this category Nicholas Kepros gave a brilliant audition). We placed great stress on intelligence, wit and humour. We thought that Hamlet should be on the small side—it is implied in the text—he does not need to be a raving masculine beauty, but, since the audience has to spend a great part of a long evening in his company, a degree of charm and magnetism is essential.

We had seen and admired a young actor in **Who's Afraid of Virginia Woolf?** His part, though long, was not a very good one. But he listened marvellously; when he spoke, the colour of his voice immediately compelled attention. He was small, lithe, elegantly put together, obviously rhythmic. To our surprise he came, uninvited, to see us. He would like to go to Minneapolis. Yes, he had been in some classical plays with A.P.A. No; no Shakespeare. No, he had never spoken verse; he had never really considered the problems. Surely, he would give an audition, but let no one expect very much.

We were impressed. He was intelligent. He was witty. He was modest. He could suggest a prince. He would obviously give his eye teeth to have a shot at Hamlet.

At the audition we tried him high. We asked him to read Hamlet's first encounter with the Ghost, one of the most difficult scenes to "feel" and also an extremely tricky scene technically. He read it without feeling, without rhythm, without artifice, but without pretension. The voice was weak, harsh and piched too high. He had no idea of how, or when, or why to breathe. He was so sensible and realistic that we did not attempt to beat about the bush. We told him what he already knew, that he had everything to learn about verse-speaking. We told him, in all sincerity, that we thought he had remarkable possibilities. We asked for time to think the matter over. He was pleasant, reasonable and seemed able—not the most usual quality in actors—to see the matter from a point of view other than that of his own immediate advantage.

It seemed to us that he had many of the assets needed for Hamlet, which are inborn and cannot be acquired; and that the assets which he lacked were of the kind which can be achieved by work. To be sure, no teacher can turn a bad voice into a good one; but a clever teacher and an earnest pupil can make a bad voice **seem** to be a good one by the skill with which it is used. In our Hamlet's case the voice is small and of

limited range, but is evidently the instrument of a lively
and interesting personality. Training can enlarge both
the volume and the compass of such a voice and can
make it an instrument, which expresses more consciously and with more control, the intentions of its pos-
sessor.

A few days later we met again and we offered
him the part, on condition that he would immediately
start singing lessons and learn as much as he could
about the vocal mechanism, and practise daily. He
agreed; and also agreed to play Solyony, the psycho-
pathic major in **The Three Sisters,** and a very small part
indeed in **The Miser.** His name, by the way, is George
Grizzard.

By now our programme had been agreed. We
would open with **Hamlet,** practically uncut; an indication, we hoped, that the audience was being regarded
as fully adult and willing to make a considerable effort
of concentration, was not being condescended to and
treated as if not fully witted, merely because Minneapolis has the misfortune to be so far from Broadway.

Hamlet would be succeeded, on the following
night, by **The Miser** of Molière, in a highly stylized production by Douglas Campbell. A few weeks after that,
as soon in fact as we could prepare it, we would offer
The Three Sisters of Chekhov; and a month later Arthur
Miller's **Death of a Salesman.** This, we hoped, would
make a clear, if implicit, statement of policy; three in-
disputable masterpieces from three widely different
cultures and three widely different epochs; each
directed in a markedly different style from the others.
The fourth play was chosen because it was American
and, in our view, a very strong contender for eventual
classical status.

Hume Cronyn would play Harpagon, in **The Miser;**

Willy Loman in **Death of a Salesman;** and the good, but
not leading, part of the Doctor in **The Three Sisters.**
Jessica Tandy would play the Queen in **Hamlet;** Mrs.
Loman; and Olga, the eldest of the Three Sisters, the
key role of that play.

By now we had engaged a strong and interesting
group of men; all had had good and varied experience
in the theatre and were, in our estimation, tempera-
mentally and technically equipped to tackle a serious
and demanding programme. We were especially happy
that John Cromwell and his wife, Ruth Nelson, were
willing to join us. Both have had distinguished careers
both on the stage and in Hollywood. They were willing
to play minor roles, in order to be part of what they
considered a valuable idea. For a repertory company
to have supporting players of this calibre is extremely
rare. Usually the smaller senior parts are played by
eighteen-year-olds in white wigs, their dear, innocent
faces cross-hatched with painted wrinkles.

So far, however, we had found no satisfactory
younger ladies. Considering how many hundreds of
talented and beautiful young women are dying to be
heard as professional actresses, you may think that this
was odd. The fact is that there is almost no opportunity
for all these girls to learn how to act.

Every modern play has a part or two for young
misses, in which they are required to be attractive and
decorative but no more. Between these sorts of parts
and important, difficult, leading parts there is a great
gap. Youngsters are very rarely cast for leading parts,
because they have neither the experience, the authority
or the Name.

The young men fare better. There are, nearly
always, even in modern plays, more male parts than

female. And the parts tend to be more interesting and demanding, to offer to those who play them a chance to develop and grow. In the classical theatre the disparity between the males and females is even more marked. In Shakespeare, for instance, there are fifteen men's parts to every woman's. And, again, the young men can gradually progress from very small, through gradually larger parts to leading young parts; from Bernardo, to Rosencrantz, to Laertes, to Hamlet. For the young women, on the other hand, there is almost no gradual progression; there are walk-ons, gentlewomen with one great line, such as "Ay, Madam"; and then Ophelia, Desdemona, Portia, Rosalind, which demand an experience, accomplishment and authority which young actresses have practically no chance to acquire.

In French and Greek classical tragedy there is the same enormous gulf fixed between tiny parts for young girls and parts like Phèdre, Medea, Alcestis, which demand great, white, spouting lady-whales. Molière is kinder to the young ladies. He offers a fine range of parts which are rewarding but still within the grasp of inexperienced youth. But amongst the great dramatists he is, in this respect, the great exception.

We saw literally hundreds of young women. Practically none of them seemed to us to have the makings of a classical actress. There were masses of bouncing sexpots—just the ticket for musicals, where it does not matter if their voices are as brassy as their hair. The young ladies who seemed to have "serious" aspirations mostly came in beatnik uniform and had tried really hard to make themselves unattractive: thick black stockings; grubby skirts of just the wrong length, droopy at the seat; grubby, art-student sweatshirts; cosmetic dog-

dirt on their lips; and on their sad little eyes a heavy
smear of greasy black. Few of these lassies spoke above
a whisper; their walk was languid; their single gesture
was to push aside with dirty hands the dirty hair which
fell across their mouths and eyes.

One such came to us with a really brilliant recom-
mendation from a previous employer whose judgement
we trusted. She was, in his opinion, the most potentially
important young actress in America. She arrived an
hour late and announced that she felt too ill to give an
audition. We made sympathetic noises and arranged to
hear her some days later. She again arrived an hour
late; she had prepared no piece, felt far too nervous to
read, but thought she might try to sing. She sang extremely well—an interesting, well-produced mezzo, with
great variety of colour.

Luckily we did not have to decide whether it was
worthwhile to cope with a neurotic and ill-disciplined
girl who might, certainly might, have extraordinary
talent. Her agent called next day to say that she was
not available; she did not wish to leave New York,
where she had just landed an important part.

It is only fair to add that her career has never
looked back and that her talent is considerable.

Eventually, for the young girl parts we engaged
Ellen Geer. I think she was, literally, the only young
actress we saw who seemed to have a fresh, healthy,
hearty happiness about her. She had a maturity, sym-
pathy and power beyond her nineteen years. Like Grizzard, she had everything to learn vocally; like him, she
was neither too proud nor too dull to learn.

For slightly more mature and "dark" parts, notably
Masha in **The Three Sisters,** we engaged Rita Gam. She
has had quite a distinguished career in movies, and her

lack of stage experience was offset partly by her striking physical beauty and partly by qualities of grit and
character, which we all learned to respect and like.

Two parts remained uncast, that of Frosine, the
scheming matchmaker in **The Miser,** and Natasha, the
humble neighbour of **The Three Sisters,** who marries
their brother and finally, like a cuckoo, shoulders the
other birds out of the nest. For these parts we wanted
Zoe Caldwell, a brilliant young Australian, whose work
we had admired very much at the English and Canadian
Stratfords. Since she is a foreign actress, permission for
her engagement had to be sought from Equity. This was
refused. The council's argument was that these were
parts for which we could certainly find an American
actress; that Miss Caldwell's engagement would only be
justified if she were a star. None of the members had
ever seen or even heard of Miss Caldwell. Several of
them, I suspect, had never heard of Australia. Our con-
tention was that we had tried and failed to find an
American actress who would play these parts as well
as Miss Caldwell; it was in the interest of Equity as well
as ourselves that the project should succeed, and success was largely conditional upon our being able to
cast the plays to what **we** considered the best advantage. Since we were offering employment to thirty-four
members of Equity, we did not think it unwarranted to
ask for the services of one foreign actress.

Equity refused to budge. Meantime, in all innocence, we had made application to the Immigation
Office, which is in St. Paul, for Zoe Caldwell to cross the
border from Canada. Applications by foreign actors to
enter the United States are submitted by the immigration authorities of New York and Chicago for endorse-
ment by Equity. It is apparently unheard-of for actors

to enter by any other channel. The immigration officer
in St. Paul had never heard of Equity. Again in all
innocence, he admitted Miss Caldwell without consulting
Equity. Once admitted apparently she was free to work.
Bureaucracy moves, like Almighty God, in a mysterious
way its wonders to perform.

We were able demurely to inform Equity that Miss
Caldwell had been granted permission to enter the
country and accept her engagement. Equity took this
not very important defeat with a furious gnashing of
collective teeth. Miss Caldwell had a smashing success
in Minneapolis. Everyone lived happily ever after.

Our company was reinforced by a dozen McKnight
Fellows. The McKnight Foundation had contributed, if
not spectacularly, to the theatre building fund, but its
main support of the project was to endow these Fellow-
ships, whereby selected graduates in drama should be
enabled to do half a year of postgraduate work in the
Drama Department of the University of Minnesota, followed by a season of practical work at the Tyrone
Guthrie Theatre.

Of the first year's McKnight Fellows, six were apprentice actors and two actresses; there were an apprentice playwright, two apprentice designers and one
man who was concerned with theatrical promotion and
management. I am happy to report that the plan
worked admirably. The twelve Fellows professed themselves satisfied with their experience and we were more
than satisfied with the service they gave.

The scheme was an imaginative idea on the part
of Walter Trenerry, the President of the McKnight Foundation. First, it makes easier for the Fellows the very
difficult and hazardous first plunge from the heated
pool of the academic theatre into the chilly and turbu-

lent ocean of the professional stage. Second, it re-
dounds to the advantage of the university Drama
Department, in as much as, so far, this is the only plan
of its kind; consequently talented young people who
want to make a start in the professional theatre will
tend to be drawn to the university which offers such an
opportunity. This should improve the level of talent in
the department without depressing its standards of
scholarship. Third, for our theatre, the services of
twelve well-educated, gifted and eager young people
were available through the generosity of the McKnight
Foundation.

But, more important in the long run than any of
these practical advantages, this scheme suggests a possible way in which the great gulf fixed between the
professional and the academic theatres may be bridged.
The bridge has been possible in this case not only
because of the grant from the Foundation, but also because the individuals concerned with making the scheme
work—the Professor of Drama and his staff, the President and Board of Regents of the university and the
board and staff of the theatre—were eager that it
should work and agreed with Mr. Trenerry that the
scheme has important, if still somewhat vague, possibilities.

We all feel that it would be unwise to set up doctrinaire regulations, or a more precise constitution than
is absolutely necessary. The vital thing is that we should
all try to see one another's points of view and feel the
way gradually into a more permanent alliance. For
our part, we of the theatre regard it as one of the elements in our project which has the most significant and
far-reaching possibilities.

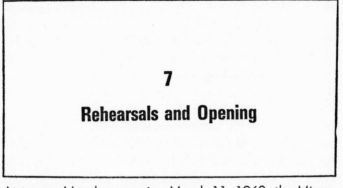

7
Rehearsals and Opening

At ten on Monday morning March 11, 1963, the Minnesota Theatre Company met in the rehearsal room of the theatre. We were quite a large group—thirty-five actors; the stage manager, Rex Partington, and his two assistants; Tanya Moiseiwitsch and her two attendants; the McKnight Fellows; Douglas Campbell and myself; and, in addition, ten men and two women, hired locally, who were to be courtiers, soldiers, and so on, in **Hamlet.**

The model of the set for **Hamlet** was on view, also the sketches for the dresses—modern dresses. Miss Moiseiwitsch and I had decided to dress this production as though the play were taking place in a contemporary European royal court. Since this decision aroused some controversy, I shall briefly explain our reasons.

In modern clothes it is possible at a glance to infer a number of things about the characters of the play, which are not apparent in period dress; the time of day, for instance, and the weather; who is a civilian and who a soldier.

The time of day is particularly important in the middle section of the play. It is valuable for the audience to realise that there is no time lapse from Hamlet's advice to the Players, right through the play scene and the subsequent scenes in the King's room and the Queen's, the chase through the palace after Hamlet

has murdered Polonius, the meeting hastily convened
by Claudius just before dawn when Hamlet is sent to
England, right through to the final scene of this se-
quence (Act 4, Scene IV), where in the first light of dawn
Hamlet, escorted by Rosencrantz and Guildenstern,
encounters, on his way to take ship for England, the
invading army of Fortinbras. All these events occur during one terrible night. This dramatic point does not
really emerge when the players are in "costume," but
in modern dress it is clear. We see them change for the
play into spectacular and elaborate evening dresses.
Not only does this mark the time of day, it also implies
that the Command Performance of **The Murder of Gon-
zago** is a Gala Occasion. During the following scenes
of confusion and panic, the finery gradually falls apart
—hair gets ruffled, ties crumple; when Claudius calls up
his "wisest friends" the hour of the day is indicated,
and the emergency stressed, by the fact that some of
them have obviously just been dug up out of their beds.

This is but one instance of many where we believed
that contemporary clothes could help to clarify a complicated story. Since we knew that a large proportion
of our audience would be seeing the play for the first
time, it seemed a good idea to make the story as clear
as we could.

This clarity might, admittedly, be achieved at the
expense of romance. To many people a great part of
their enjoyment of Shakespeare derives from the picturesque charm of fancy dress. For them it matches the
picturesque charm of fancy language.

This was a view of Shakespeare which we were not
eager to encourage. His language is not primarily picturesque and charmingly olde-world. Its high colour and
the fact that here and there he uses a word which has

either become obsolete or somewhat changed in meaning must not be allowed to obscure the clarity and force of the writing. His characters are not fairy-tale characters. They are portraits of real men and women by a great master of accurate observation and shrewd comment. The fact that they frequently express themselves in rhetorical blank verse rather than in realistic prose must not obscure the accuracy or blur the shrewdness. The great Shakespearian creations are all a good deal larger, more high-coloured and more articulate than the people we habitually meet on the subway and in the supermarket. That should not, however, cause us to interpret them romantically. But unless we are extremely careful that is exactly what we all do.

Theatre audiences have an almost incurable tendency to romanticize. They long to transform every good-looking young actor into a Hero, and every good-looking young actress into a Heroine. Heroes, as everyone knows, are brave, incorruptible and chivalrous; they may not legitimately get angry, even violent, with wrongdoers; to women they are invariably kind and gentle, but not so gentle that it is not gratifying for the feminine members of the audience to see them Tamed by Love. Heroines must, of course, be pretty, but above all they must be pure. They need not be a bit clever or useful or amusing. In plays, heroines' purity is quite often "smirched" or "spotted"; never, of course, through their own fault; they have been Wronged by a Wicked Man.

The less good-looking young men and women have to be content with "character parts," which means that they must be a bundle of eccentric mannerisms. Some of the character parts are servants, in which case they must either be faithful or comic. It is rather popular

when, in a play, a comic servant unexpectedly turns out
to be faithful as well. Older people, if they play leading parts, are broadly classified as Good and Bad.
Senior people who play smaller parts are also "character."

These romantic stereotypes are what all of us instinctively look for in the theatre, indeed in fiction of
all types. When we go to **Hamlet** our natural inclination
is to believe that Hamlet is the hero (darkly poetical,
Byronic); Ophelia is the heroine (blonde and pure); the
King and Queen are "heavies" (Mr. and Mrs. Vincent
Crummles); Polonius is First Comic Character Gentleman, the Gravedigger is Second Comic Character
Gentleman. Everything is good and obvious. We have
nothing more to do but to munch the candy, which
Mavis has so thoughtfully brought in nice rustly paper,
and to note, as they pass by, the quotations—"to thine
own self be true . . . something is rotten in the state of
Denmark . . . for thine especial safety" and, at long
last, "Good night, sweet prince."

Perhaps it is impertinent, but as a Director I feel it
is my duty to try to protect Shakespeare, and to try to
protect all of us, from our passionate addiction to
Romance and to Stereotype.

Therefore in **Hamlet** it seemed a good idea to dress
the characters in a manner which accords with the text
but does not necessarily accord with the stereotype.

How, it may be argued, can a modern-dress production accord with a text which describes Hamlet as
appearing to Ophelia with "his doublet all unbraced,
no hat upon his head, his stockings fouled, ungartered
and down-gyved to his ankle." It cannot. But this, I
think, is the single instance where modern dress does
not support the text; and to condemn the use of modern

dress simply for this one departure does not seem reasonable, if it be admitted that there are adequate compensatory reasons for its use.

I suppose the arch-stereotype of all theatrical stereotypes is the figure of Hamlet himself. I would venture to assume that for most people the name Hamlet conjures up a vision of a very mournful, distempered-looking young person in a black velvet tam-o'-shanter with a drooping ostrich feather, black velvet tunic trimmed with black beads, black tights. The figure is addressing itself to a skull. It is the incarnation of the Gloomy Dane and derives, I suspect, from numerous engravings of old actors in the role.

In fact, to my mind, the evidence that Hamlet is a gloomy fellow, who is "constitutionally incapable of decisive action," is entirely outweighed by contrary evidence in the text. Further, there is no reason to suppose that the "traditional" costume is any more right than a modern suit, rather the contrary. The "traditional" black bonnet and tunic does not accord with the costume worn in Shakespeare's own day, nor with the textual evidence of doublet, stockings, garters and so on. There is reason to believe, though no one knows for certain, that Burbage, the original interpreter of Hamlet, will, according to theatrical custom of his day, have worn contemporary dress, to which will have been added a certain amount of fancywork and feathers to denote royalty and make a show.

There would therefore be some logic in producing the play in late Elizabethan dress. This is very rarely done, for several excellent reasons. If the clothes of this period are to look either authentic or handsome, they must be made of very stiff, heavy and expensive material; they demand a high degree of craftsmanship from the tailor and an inordinate amount of his time; they need a great deal of maintenance and laundry work; and, when finally achieved, are exceedingly uncomfortable and difficult to wear.

Failing Elizabethan dress, it seems to me that modern clothes are the next most logical choice, though I admit logic is not necessarily the right basis for deciding how to dress a play.

The "traditional" costume is not logical at all; it is based upon styles seen in early sixteenth-century Italian painting, which are then freely adapted to suit the figure of the actor, the taste of the designer and the purse of the management. There are, however, good arguments in its favour; it is cheap, comfortable, becoming and, because it is so usual in the context of **Hamlet,** it excites no undue comment, it is accepted as "right." The single good reason against using it seems to me unanswerable; it encourages the audience, almost obliges it, to accept the romantic stereotype.

We figured that if the characters looked recognisable, like the sort of people with whom we are familiar and whom we can place in the context of our own experience, it would be easier to accept them as real people, not just as remote beings from another era. We believed that by so doing we need not necessarily make the stage look drab and ordinary. The fact that the play is set in a royal court permitted us to dress the men either in formal clothes or handsome, colourful full-dress uniforms, and to deck the women out with long gloves, plenty of jewelry and dignified, long dresses. Some of our critics objected that the full-dress uniforms were nineteenth-century and did not "go" with modern civilian suits. In this they were mistaken. In all European courts, military full dress has hardly changed in the last hundred years, and is seen in the same rooms and at the same functions as completely modern civilian clothes.

Our final reason for producing this particular **Hamlet** in modern dress was that we believed it would better suit an American cast, less at home with "period" plays than British actors who get more opportunities to appear in them. American actors are apt to be inhibited and self-conscious in the clothes of other days. They feel that they must grope for something called "style," which consists of getting into elegant attitudes, tapping snuffboxes, waving fans and lace handkerchiefs and in general carrying-on in a very fancy way. In fact, style is not something which can be assumed externally. It consists of knowledge, of knowing what the play you are doing is about, which involves not just a knowledge of the story and the characters but of their whole environment. Only so can you be sure of why your speeches are written as they are, why your character behaves as he does; only in the light of such knowledge can you wear your clothes, move, speak, think and feel truly. Style, therefore, in a period play is the knowledge which enables your acting to bear the stamp of truth.

Moreover, style does not only apply to period plays, or to plays about grand and elegant people. There is a style to Westerns, for instance, which totally eludes British actors, but comes easily to actors who have the right knowledge; the knowledge, in this case, of the relevant environment. If competent British actors can make the complete hash, which I have seen them do, of **Oklahoma!** or **Room Service,** it ought not to be strange if no less competent American actors approach Shakespeare with the accent on values other than Renaissance splendour and high style.

In taking the decision to produce **Hamlet** in this manner, we realised that we should incur a great deal of disapproval. Many otherwise reasonable people simply cannot believe that modern-dress Shakespeare is intended to be taken seriously, that it is not intended to be either funny or naughtily sensational.

Reason hardly enters into this matter; furious passion is aroused; and in my experience women feel it far more strongly than men. Can it be that their anger is a manifestation of the Father-complex? Shakespeare is the Father-figure and those who "interfere with" or "belittle" his work are insulting Father. Perhaps this may seem far-fetched but I cannot otherwise account for the irrationally angry tone of certain press critics and also private correspondents. Similar rage has been aroused by every Shakespearian production which I have attempted in any style of dress other than traditional "renaissance type"; moreover, when Michael Langham staged an extremely fine **Coriolanus** in dress of the French First Empire there was a similar irrational explosion of anger.

I have digressed at some length on this matter because it seems relevant in any consideration of a classical repertoire. If classics are to be fresh and not preserved in a sort of aspic of uncritical reverence, then there must be constant experiment with their production. Yet it must be faced that such experiment will be conducted in the teeth of furious opposition by a considerable section of just that public who will be the support of a classic theatre. It is a pity in some ways; but on the whole I welcome such opposition. It is a sign of life. Controversy is far healthier than acquiescence.

I can see reason in the argument that a classical theatre should perform a service analogous to that of

an art museum, that a selection of dramatic masterpieces should be constantly available **in traditional
style.**

The problem is that in drama, as in music, there
is wide disagreement about what constitutes traditional
style; it is even arguable that such a style does not
exist. Music and drama are performing arts. The writers'
and composers' work requires interpretation by other
artists. Every such interpretation must necessarily be a
comment. It cannot simply realise the composers' or
writers' intention without comment. Lively comment is
apt to be controversial and conspicuous; inconspicuous
comments which arouse no controversy are apt to be
dull. A classical theatre, where the productions were accepted without controversy, would not, in my estimation,
be performing so valuable a service as a theatre where
the productions caused some stir.

For some weeks we had watched in a fever of
impatience the apparently snail-like progress of the
work on the building. This was the third time I had been
connected with the opening of a new theatre, and Peter
Zeisler had nightmare memories of the opening at
Stratford, Connecticut. We tried to restrain our anxiety,
tried not to carry mentally every hod, pour every square
inch of concrete, hammer every nail and plaster every
crack. In the theatre you just have to be ready on opening night or bust. There can be no excuses, no evasions.
If the performance isn't ready, the ship goes down with
all hands. In the construction business there exist, apparently, no such ineluctable deadlines. In my simplicity
I had always supposed that there was something called
a Penalty Clause, under which, if the building was not
ready by the promised date, vast sums had to be

coughed up . . . by whom? I found I was far from clear about the whole business and so, apparently, was our building committee, whose members were no less agitated than ourselves and equally helpless.

Our rehearsals were not as badly thrown out of gear as we had expected by the building not being ready. For the first two or three weeks the stage was not available; but in the first weeks that did not really matter. The rehearsal room offered adequate space, though it is a cheerless, chilly, unattractive chamber.

We had allowed eight weeks between the first rehearsal and the opening. During that time **Hamlet** and **The Miser** had to be prepared. It so happened we had allowed a needlessly long time and were able to give the company a brief "recess" at Easter.

Hamlet is rather a quick play to rehearse. Most of the scenes are conducted between quite small groups of two or three or four; there are only three big ensembles, including the finale, which is shorter and very much easier to arrange than most of Shakespeare's big finales. George Grizzard had arrived in Minneapolis ten days ahead of the rest of the company and he and I had done a great deal of groundwork, exchanging ideas, reaching agreement about the interpretation and working in detail upon the speaking of the soliloquys.

The Miser needed more time. The meaning of the play offers considerably less field for exploration and argument than does the meaning of **Hamlet,** but technically it makes great demands. Douglas Campbell's production laid great stress upon choreography. It was almost a dance to the accompaniment of a spoken score. To many of the actors this was something quite new. Here, they thought, is style with a vengeance. They saw the designs for the costumes—pastel-coloured, frilly, flouncy and derivative from the commedia dell' arte. They started fanning and fluttering and carrying on to beat the band, till Campbell, who was directing and who is less like a ballet master than anyone could possibly be, beat the hell out of everyone who tried to be dainty. Drawings by Daumier were passed about and there was talk on the lines of: "It's perfectly possible to be rhythmic without a change of sex."

We rehearsed day and day about, at first for about six hours, later for longer. In addition to the rehearsals for the two opening plays, there was a daily movement class conducted by Campbell. This was voluntary. But practically everyone attended with admirable constancy, except John Cromwell and myself, who were too old and decrepit for the very strenuous manoeuvres involved. It was part-dancing, part-gym, part breathing. The idea was to release tension and give everyone a good stretch and a deep breath as a prelude to the more cerebral efforts of rehearsal.

Then there were fencing classes. These were intended primarily for Hamlet and Laertes and their understudies, and at first revolved around the complicated routine of their duel in the finale of **Hamlet.** But gradually quite a number of the actors, women as well as men, took the class, partly to learn the elements of the art of fencing, partly for the pleasure of the strenuous exercise.

In addition, on most days, right after the movement class, I used to rehearse the whole company for twenty minutes or so in the choral speaking of the 118th Psalm. This was partly to prepare it for the Service of Dedication which was to open the theatre, and partly to try to get us all thinking along broadly similar lines, and talking a broadly similar language, about the speaking of words.

I think we all enjoyed these classes and that they

were valuable in bringing us together and making us
feel a united group. Technically they were not of enormous importance, though each of them contributed
something. The important thing was that for an hour or
so every day we all did something together and on
terms of equality.

On Sunday, May 5, the theatre was opened with
a religious Service of Dedication. A Lutheran minister,
a Jewish rabbi and a Catholic priest were on the platform. The service was non-denominational, brief and
very simple. The excellent choir of one of the Lutheran
churches in Minneapolis led the congregation in two
hymns and also sang anthems by Schubert and
Gretchaninoff very splendidly; the four trumpeters and
the tympanist, who are the theatre's resident musicians,
played pieces by Bach and Gretchaninoff and the
actors spoke the psalm, which we had been rehearsing,
very splendidly. The house was by no means full but I
think that most of the six or seven hundred people
present found it a very moving occasion. That night
and the following night there were "preview" performances of **The Miser** and **Hamlet** before invited audiences.

Tuesday, May 7, was the date of the first public
performance. **Hamlet** was the play. It was a highly
social occasion. Everyone who was Anyone in the Twin
Cities was present in full regalia. The cast was dread-
fully nervous but not, I believe, so nervous as the audience, which was highly conscious of the significance of
the occasion and perhaps also a little conscious of the
hordes of newsmen and women with their satellite
photographers. The tension at the beginning was extreme, far too much to be wholesome. To make matters
worse, the thermometer that evening had leapt up

twenty or thirty degrees. Instead of ordinary agreeable May weather, midsummer heat seemed suddenly to have been switched on. In addition to being sickeningly nervous, we were all sickeningly hot.

At this point I realised with painful clarity just what a risk we had taken by opening with **Hamlet.** In theory it seemed sound enough. To open with the most famous and interesting play in the world would proclaim our classical policy; would proclaim that there would be no condescension because we were in the upper Midwest, not in New York. But in practice here we had on our hands an audience which was obviously not the audience upon which we should, if we survived, depend for support. This was overwhelmingly a "fashionable" audience, drawn by the occasion, not by any desire to see a great tragedy. It also included several hundred newspaper people, not just critics, but columnists and gossip writers, not the easiest crowd to move to enthusiasm or from whom to wring a tear. The presence of all these could have been foreseen. What, however, was so disconcerting was the excitement, the tension.

What this audience at this moment **wanted** was a bullfight, or a belly dancer going **far** too far, or two heavyweights bashing the daylights out of each other; anything to release the tension and provoke great tremors of excited response. Why, oh why, could we not have foreseen this? What they were going to be asked to give was four hours of solid, concentrated attention.

After six minutes, some of the sillier Society Ladies began fidgeting with their scarves and admiring their own rings and necklaces; after ten, the coughing began; after twenty, it was very clear that the excitement had evaporated and the battle to win the attention which the play demands had been lost.

I still do not know whether **Hamlet,** almost uncut,

was an unwise choice for the opening programme. No great play would have stood a chance that night. The audience wanted excitement, excitement, excitement. And yet if we had fobbed them off with a heavily cut and more exciting version, or had presented a sort of pot-pourri of Gems from the Classic Drama, with the leading players doing brief, effective showpieces, the society ladies would have had a less arduous evening, but the serious supporters and the press would rightly have felt insulted.

I hope that I have not implied that this First Night was worse than any other. It was miserable, but then, Openings, or anyway, Openings of important and difficult plays, which demand something more than that the audience be excited or amused, always are miserable.

This misery cannot, I guess, be avoided. It is needful, apparently, that Opening Nights should be "fashionable," only so do they register in the newspapers, and other media of information, as important. Newspaper readers and television viewers like, apparently, to learn that Mrs. Smucker was present in heliotrope slipper satin and that Mrs. Gunk wore the Gunk rubies.

This creates a sense of occasion.

The Smuckers and the Gunks, however, are not a representative audience. They are very rich and very eager to be seen at a Cultural Occasion, if it is being highly publicised. Of **Hamlet** and such stuff they know little and care less. To help them through a terrible evening they are apt to dine well. They therefore arrive a little overexcited and, by half way through the first act, reaction sets in. Mr. Smucker is only kept upright in his seat by the surreptitious nudges and kicks of his better half; when Mrs. Gunk makes to snore, Gunk fetches her a good whack on the rubies. None of this makes things easy for the actors, who are nervous anyway. It is a pity therefore that this is the performance which is seen by the professional critics; that this is the performance about which they record their impression for the public. The impression cannot but be a distorted one.

I guess the misery must be endured in order to achieve the Sense of Occasion. I sometimes wonder if it is not achieved at too high a cost.

The Miser on the next evening fared better. For one thing, because it was the second, not the first, night the Occasion did not so completely overwhelm the play, for another, it is shorter, lighter and funnier than **Hamlet.** The cast was again, and naturally, nervous, which meant that the peripheral fancywork tended to dominate the central story. The performance that night was rather like a song with a very elaborate accompaniment which the pianist, through nervousness, plays too loud and too fast.

I shall not attempt any assessment of the performances of our four plays. Clearly I could not be impartial. For those who are interested to read how they were received, I include, with their writers' permission, some of the press notices.

The stage seemed to us to work with remarkable versatility. We had been nervous about how **The Three Sisters** would fare upon an open stage. In fact, I did not hear of anyone being bothered about this, except Nathan Cohen of the "Toronto Star," a critic who is rather easily bothered by any innovation. Miss Moiseiwitsch designed the production so that the actors were not isolated from their background, but the background was perforce a little more sketchy than in a proscenium theatre. On balance, however, I believe that the more sketchy background was offset by more natural grouping and more intimate contact with the audience. The bedroom (Act 3) was the least satisfactory setting. In a proscenium it could have been more confined, which would have been better—we had too much space—and the lighting could have been more atmospheric. On the other hand, the last act, which Chekhov sets in a garden, never seems satisfactory in a proscenium, which can cope with realistic interiors but is nearly always defeated by outdoor effects unless they can be shrouded in tactful darkness. On our stage, however, the exterior scene was neither more nor less realistic than the interiors. The style, I thought, was maintained more consistently than is possible in a proscenium.

We did not entirely conquer acoustic problems. In certain parts of the house the actors are not adequately heard. I do not think that this responsibility can be laid at the door of the architect. For a house which holds nearly fifteen hundred people the acoustics are remarkably good. The fault, I fear, lies with us—the directors and actors. On an open stage an actor must speak extra clearly. This is partly because his voice is being directed away from some of his listeners, and partly because, since the same people cannot see his face, they cannot, as we all do perhaps more than we realise, eke out by lip-reading. We found it rather tempting, because the distance from a speaker to the back of the house is so very much less than in a proscenium theatre of similar capacity, to act and direct too intimately. It is fair, however, to assume that with more experience of this theatre we shall learn to use it better. Even an experienced operator takes a while to get the hang of a new machine.

Since it would obviously be unsuitable for me, or any of us immediately concerned, to assess the quality of the first season's productions, there now follows a selection of press critiques.

It will be obvious that I have not selected just the most favourable. Some were better than these, none worse than that written by Claudia Cassidy.

In what follows, the critics' notices are quoted in full. Not every word, written in the context of a particular moment, is now relevant. But to omit passages can only give the impression that the "nastier" bits have been suppressed. It has for too long been a managerial practice to quote only the favorable parts of a critique. Thus a critic may have written: "Miss B. is handsome and her performance would have been less unsatisfactory had it matched her appearance." Without altering a word, the management quotes this as: "Miss B. is handsome and . . . her performance matched her appearance."

Walter Kerr on **Hamlet** from "New York Herald Tribune," May 9, 1963:

We are accustomed to seeing all of the seats in the theater the same color, and there is no particular reason why they should look like a crazy quilt of jostling pastels, with yellows and blues and oranges contending for elbow room—except that, as it happens, they look gayer that way.

There is no particular reason why a two-million-dollar playhouse with two exterior faces (one glass, one wood, both with multiple eyes) and with an interior resembling a waxed and polished prize ring should have been imagined, financed, built and fed with actors in Minneapolis, Minnesota—except that Minneapolis just decided to go ahead and do it.

Nor is there any entirely sane reason why director Tyrone Guthrie should have thought actor George Grizzard ready to play *Hamlet*, except that (a) Mr. Grizzard is one of the finest young actors in the country, and (b) ready or not, if he doesn't do it now, he never will.

As of Tuesday evening, Mr. Guthrie, Mr. Grizzard, Minneapolis and an architect with holes in his façade all said, "What have we got to lose, except money and our reputations?" And went for broke. They won't go broke. They'll probably go to heaven for their nerve, cheek, faith, recklessness, impracticality and wisdom, with no more than a month or two in purgatory for the sins they haven't bothered to avoid.

The occasion is exciting because it just plain doesn't care about anything except the right to work. Mr. Guthrie doesn't care about time, in any of its possible senses. His new *Hamlet* is more than four hours long, and seems so. It also uses candles and flashlights in the very same castle, just as it uses rapiers in one scene and revolvers in the next. The night watch on the ramparts wear costumes out of Graustark, Hamlet returns from England in a curled-wool cap that suggests an impending mission to Moscow, and between times we are eavesdropping on a patent-leather Polonius.

Does the circus-on-a-clothesline spirit do any damage to Shakespeare? Sometimes yes. To see Ham-

let captured by a posse carrying flashlights suggests
that he has been misbehaving in a movie theatre and
has been rounded up by the ushers. And there is no
need for Claudius to sneak the bullets out of the gun
Laertes has been waving around; we know Claudius
was a villain all the time. But out of all the free inven-
tion Mr. Guthrie gets another effect—the effect of
looking at the entire play naked, of watching its bones
dance on the graveside, or hearing what it is saying
without quite remembering that it is old.

And there are typical Guthrie improvisations that
work most wonderfully. Two doors closing firmly in
Hamlet's face as he means to follow his mother from
the court. A buzz of spectators catching the implications of the play-within-a-play long before Claudius
lets his own nerves be shown; the grapevine runs
ahead of the guilty man. John Cromwell, as the Player
King, threatening to quit in splendid petulance when
Polonius suggests he has gone on too long. (And
ironically, Mr. Cromwell is the only Player King who
did not seem to go on too long.) Jessica Tandy, as
Gertrude, standing directly beside the ghost she
cannot see, the husband she chooses not to remember;
or again, Miss Tandy reporting Ophelia's death, and
moving away from us all, a vanishing stalk of gray,
as though she were going to say nothing more as long
as she lived.

There is a Ghost (Ken Ruta) who whispers of
poison poured in an ear, while whispering poison into
Hamlet's ear. There is an Ophelia (Ellen Geer) who
redeems the vocal monotony of her earlier distress
with the scratched-nails groveling of her madness. Lee
Richardson makes an oily tycoon-in-trouble out of
Claudius. Ed Prebble reads the live-and-let-die philosophy of his gravedigger perfectly; Graham Browne

is an impassioned rather than a passive Horatio. But
we are keeping Mr. Grizzard waiting, and not waiting,
at center stage. To him.

The first word of his performance is cautious, as
though he thought he would be sent home if he did
not get each line-reading right. In this mood, he offers
us the intelligence of the words, but leaves his own
quick actor's intelligence—his alertness, his liveliness,
his swiftness of response—in the dressing room. He
is never surprised; he knows the lines too well. With
the arrival of the Players, though, something happens
to him; one feels he has found friends. Actors are actors, after all, and why not just go ahead and be one?

By the time of the closet scene his instincts have
taken command, he is direct, abandoned, pressing—
and lo and behold, his voice has caught up with him
and is penetrating too. The scene lives in its own right
—so firmly, in fact, that the "guts" of Polonius can
be disposed of in a most unembarrassed fashion. Mr.
Grizzard is not at present holding his gains: en route
to England he has become fuzzily reflective again. It
cannot be said that, over all, this is anything like a
mature, or fiery, or poetically free Hamlet. What can
be said is that it was entirely worth doing.

For this is the plunge, a plunge of many kinds
for many people. The theater will never get anything
done if it isn't willing to take a whack at it, and here
are talented and determined people whacking in all
directions. The score doesn't have to come out heavily
in their favor; it is the game that counts just now.

Walter Kerr on **The Miser** from "New York Herald
Tribune," May 10, 1963:

The Miser is not only funny and charming, it's
Molière. Everyone pretends to know that Molière can

be funny and charming and even more than that, of course, but it's all pretending because no one ever gets to see the man's work—not in New York, and certainly not in English.

The Tyrone Guthrie Theater has now taken care of the matter for the citizens of Minneapolis, at least, and if a rumor should begin to radiate outward from there that Molière is playable, who can tell what might not happen?

I suppose it would have been easy enough for director Douglas Campbell simply to cover the French master's ancient farce formula with an overlay of pretty posturing and an icing of whipped-cream costumes, and then let it go at that as a graceful bow to the past.

In point of fact, he hasn't neglected the foolish furbelows.

When Clayton Corzatte minces onto the vast, glittering apron stage—staff in hand and hand on heart as a foppish young lover—he looks like a cat that has taken a bad fall into a Schrafft's dessert.

John Cromwell, arriving late in the entertainment, as the man who knows the clue to everyone's identity, arrives under the shelter of a hat that would make a fine egg-salad sandwich.

Tanya Moiseiwitsch's costumes have all been made in the basement workrooms of the adventurous new playhouse, and I'd hate to be the man who's sweeping up after her.

But never mind the fleet-in-full-sail costuming or the clattering busyness that Campbell has invented to keep the half-masked servants and the half-mad lovers swooping and scurrying, counterclockwise and back, along the outer edges of the apron (there is even too much busyness but let's reserve that for the moment).

What counts, if Molière is to be served at all, is the core of the comic spirit, the not entirely antic passions that stomp and fuss and then stand stockstill at center stage.

The Miser is not merely a joke. It also takes the measure of something close to a monster, and this without losing laughter, or making the monster less than a man.

In its central role, Hume Cronyn nails the evening to the floor with the hard, brass tacks of preposterous plausibility.

He is as amusing as need be, and more. With a wispy, gray wig, a clatter of keys at his waist, and eyeglasses that seem to fold forward in concentration, he walks with the self-astonishment of an upright caterpillar, seeing to it that the servants do not serve too much for dinner and that no one wastes money on happiness.

But the portrait is richer than the thwacks with an actual slapstick or the asthma that overtakes him when he enjoys a dance step too much.

What is best in his performance is the burrowing he does with his mind. He can burrow two ways. He can almost persuade himself that he is handsome, that his young bride-to-be might adore him, that some pretty chicks really prefer disintegrating oldsters (sixty is the minimum age they set).

As he leans forward, eyes almost crossed in the effort at self-deception, mouth working steadily as though it were in training to become a steel trap, he makes a comic spectacle, something close to a specter, with absurd hope and wistfulness all mixed in.

Even so, that mind isn't napping. It can hear the faint lie behind the flattery, and with the sound of one false inflection, explode into fact-facing common sense, and full fury, once again.

It is this foundation of human cussedness—or cussed humanness—that makes possible Cronyn's transition to an almost insanely sober despair once his fortune has vanished from its hiding place in the garden.

The transition is, I think, a bit abrupt in its present staging. The lighting grows stone-cold before we have quite grasped that his heart has too.

But in the playing-out of the frenzy that follows, Cronyn meets the test that keeps turning up in Molière: Something behind the mockery really means it.

I promised to mention certain excesses and odd uses of a wide-open acting area.

One of these comes with a conceit that Campbell has adopted: Since there are no doors to this stage, masked pages are invited to stand in position and to swing in and out on entrances with a whistle and a slap accompanying each opening and closing.

And since these supers are always available, when a player has an "aside" to toss somewhere he can always direct it to them.

If both devices are at first sight engaging they are also perverse in the circumstances. For this is the very play that needs no doors, and this is the very playhouse in which "asides" can really be confided to a vast surrounding audience. Having gotten scenery out of the way, we have turned some actors into scenery.

But the objection is minor, considering the color and the substance Campbell has got into the entertainment.

If Rita Gam and Ellen Geer tend to overstress

the artifice of their romantic young ladies, Corzatte, Cromwell, and Claude Woolman know precisely how to turn a posture into a comment.

Zoe Caldwell is spectacularly good as a thoroughly unreliable matchmaker, wrapping her voice around Cronyn like the wings of dishonest angel.

And Cronyn himself has just the dimensions needed for this three-dimensional theater. No matter which way he turns, he keeps on ruling himself away.

Claudia Cassidy on **Hamlet** and **The Miser** from "Sunday Tribune," Chicago, May 19, 1963:

It was at the Edinburgh Festival of 1949 that I first encountered Tyrone Guthrie and Douglas Campbell, whose collaboration in *The Three Estates* set off the journey that blazed up at Canada's Stratford Festival ten years ago and just opened a new and so far sharply disappointing era at the Tyrone Guthrie Theatre in Minneapolis.

As I do not consider a city really civilized without such a theater on a high level, I went to Minneapolis hoping that brilliant direction could vitalize what looked from the outside like a fairly pedestrian troupe. Instead Sir Tyrone gave the crucial product a queasy start with a singularly cheapened *Hamlet*, and Mr. Campbell beat *The Miser* to a simpering froth of surface slapstick. Both plays were on the whole amateurishly acted and clumsily directed, with little indication of the freedom within disciplined form that is the basic classic style.

When I say that I was sharply disappointed, I mean precisely that. I am unable to watch two such performances with the equanimity which says, well, it isn't very good, but isn't it wonderful they are all working? Or, I wouldn't want it myself, but isn't it marvelous for Minneapolis? Or, and this catalog of extenuation could go on for pages, everything has to start somewhere—give them time. I would happily give all the time in the world to an exciting effort even if it is only getting coiled to spring. The second-rate isn't worth waiting for.

It would seem to me intolerably condescending to Minneapolis, or any other city so situated, to suggest that it has been mutually met on a high level. With the help of the Walker and Ford Foundations, Minneapolis built a handsome theater according to Guthrie specifications of outthrust stage wrapped on three sides by sharply ramped seats. Starting with the Walker grant of land and cash, Minneapolis raised more than two million dollars for the theater, and the Ford Foundation guaranteed it against loss for three years, the term of Guthrie's commitment. By opening night the ticket sale for the twenty-week summer season exceeded $300,000.

Nor was that all. The theater engaged Mary Joliffe, who had helped launch Stratford and Toronto's O'Keefe, as publicity director. Miss Joliffe is astonishing. She is so organized that she can look delightful at the end of a long, hard opening night. If your cab doesn't come she has a limousine in her pocket. Information is in your hand before you know you want it. And, whether or not it was her idea, previews were played to men who worked on the theater, and their families, and cab drivers who are the indispensable men, at least for visitors without a car.

The plays were anticlimax. Had they aimed

high, missed and fallen flat, it would have been under-
standable. The right to fail in such circumstances is the
artist's birthright. But an audience is not without rights
of its own. Specifically, it has the right to expect the
highest achievement of which a project is capable at
the moment.

The outthrust stage, which Guthrie has developed
from Edinburgh's assembly hall through Stratford in
Canada, has the possibility of swift action in its favor,
and dubious acoustics in its disfavor. It is more suited
to the theater of movement than to the theater of the
mind. But there is no denying its potential excitement.
Walk into the Minneapolis Theater with its harlequin
seat covers glowing in the high-pitched dusk, and
catch your breath. My problem was that I stayed to
yawn.

Both the Guthrie *Hamlet* and the Campbell *Miser*
are staged to throw dust in your eyes, possibly to hide
the meagerness of their acting resources. It probably
was Sandman's dust by inadvertence. Incessant, often
meaningless movement, distracting the stage business
and highly personal interpretations by the directors,
made *Hamlet* interminable and *The Miser* bumpkin
fare.

That the Campbell Molière is inept is not astonishing, as he has had limited experience in stage direction. He aims at the ebullience of commedia dell'arte
and the literal thwack of the slapstick, and winds up
doing much too much of everything, usually all at
once. The confusion is such that only so adroit a
comedienne as Zoe Caldwell, whose matchmaker
rivals Ruth Gordon's, can authoritatively cut through.
Hume Cronyn's Harpagon has quality up to a point,

with a flick of the mercurial. But this is a challenging role of many facets, designed for marvelous interplay. Except for Miss Caldwell, with whom he teams beguilingly, Cronyn is a duellist without an opponent, shorn of thrust, parry and riposte.

Tyrone Guthrie is no tyro. He often has a touch of Irish quicksilver, for all of being born at Tunbridge Wells. But many of his triumphs have been comedies. He has staged *Hamlet* infrequently in a long career.

Not long ago he was saying that, while he found Olivier the most vigorous Hamlet, Barrymore the most romantic, Evans the most consistently audible, and Plummer the wittiest, the one he likes best was Gielgud, "the most musical and the most royal."

Admittedly he had at Minneapolis no such resources. But by what antic disposition did he choose for this *Hamlet* much the same milieu which so sardonically and amusingly displaced (sic) his *Troilus and Cressida* eight or nine years ago? Both Danes and Trojans resembled the German general staff of World War I, and the epicene fops he made of Polonius and Pandarus were distinguishable chiefly by the fact that Paul Rogers, an expert actor, played Pandarus.

It is true that in both plays lechery vies with treachery, but *Troilus and Cressida* is one of "the dark plays" most of whose characters are bawds and pimps and traitors and fools. It is a difficult, little-known tragedy, and the brilliant Guthrie production, exasperating to many informed playgoers, did not obscure it, but revealed it by placing it in a different light.

The Minneapolis *Hamlet* obscures and destroys a great play. It is drab and misleading. It has misplaced the poetry that is the play's power and glory. It seeks to startle the eye by having Laertes carry tennis racquets, by putting Hamlet into business suits by a luckless tailor—the Ophelia, not having been informed, speaks on cue of his doublet and stockings —by taking Rosencrantz and Guildenstern straight out of *Waiting for Lefty.* A Claudius in a cutaway pours wine from heavy cut-glass decanters, wheeled out on a white cocktail cart.

Even more discomfiting is the way lines are thrown away or dissected for readjustment. In the "What a piece of work is man!" speech it doesn't come out "In apprehension how like a God!" It emerges or emerged, "How like an angel in apprehension (pause) / How like a God!"

Well, there it is or part of it. Antic gestures instead of the roots repertory. What subsequent productions of *The Three Sisters* (Guthrie) and *Death of a Salesman* (Campbell) can do to rescue the season, only their openings can tell. From the introductory plays I can see no company capable of doing much with Chekhov. With Cronyn and Jessica Tandy, Arthur Miller should have some luck.

But the whole thing is miles from what I mean by a resident theater worth cherishing—and a long, long way from the Tyrone Guthrie who has refreshed the theater scene for reassuring seasons.

Dan Sullivan on **The Three Sisters** from the "Minneapolis Morning Tribune," June 19, 1963:

In the library it is possible to admire Chekhov's *Three Sisters* as an accurate, clinical study of provin-

cial melancholy without caring too deeply about what
happens—or, more to the point, what doesn't happen—to its characters.

It is even possible to despise them a little as
languid, soft-shell creatures half in love with the quiet
desperation to which they are reduced.

On the stage it is the task of the director to make
us care for them—if possible to make us love them.
The glory of Tyrone Guthrie's lovely production,
which opened Tuesday night at the Guthrie Theatre,
is that we do.

Without adding a trace of spurious vitality or
cheap laughter to the play, Guthrie has given us a
double handful of men and women who, though ultimately worn down by life, have done their best (and
it is often a pitiably puny best) not to surrender.

"Ta-ra-ra-boom-de-ay" hums Hume Cronyn,
infinitely touching as the alcoholic Dr. Tchebutykin in
the last act. "It doesn't matter. It's all the same."

Then Cronyn gives a wicker chair a sullen kick,
and we see that it is not all the same. We have left
self-pity for the genuine, tragic article.

Chekhov's Three Sisters are three no-longer-
young women, who hope to find the secret of life, a
secret that so far has eluded them, in a one-way ticket
out of town.

They do not get the ticket, they do not find the
secret (unless it is that there is no secret) and in the
end, as their friends in an army regiment leave for
another post, they are left alone.

"Our life is not over yet!" says kind, faded Olga
(Jessica Tandy). We are sure she means it and, as the
lights dim, we can only hope she is right.

All of which sounds very gloomy. How, we think,

can Chekhov have described his plays as lyrical comedies?

Guthrie shows us how, for the play is drenched with affectionate laughs as these dear, silly people try to do the grand thing and only succeed in doing the usual thing.

"I love you—passionately!" prim Lieutenant Tusenbach (Claude Woolman) declaims with a flourish —which knocks his overcoat to the floor.

"What has become of my past?" wails henpecked André (Charles Cioffi) to a deaf servant (Ed Prebble) who cannot fathom his rhetoric.

Guthrie's production is a remarkably well-balanced one, marked with ensemble playing so solid that in scenes like the first-act birthday party we are not so much an audience as a collection of eavesdroppers.

If there are no stars, however, there are several fine individual performances. Rita Gam's portrayal of the discontented Masha, for example, should erase Miss Gam's movie-starlet image for all time. Ellen Geer as the youngest sister, Irina, shows us exquisitely the death of a girl and the birth of an old maid. Zoe Caldwell is properly insufferable as the vulgar sister-in-law—yet properly too she is not a villain. There are no villains in this play.

The most outstanding male characterization, next to Cronyn's, is George Grizzard's moody, sardonic Captain Solyony, of the nervous cackle. Robert Pastene, as Colonel Vershinin, gives us a philosopher, half-sick of hearing himself talk yet unable to stop (and how well Pastene manages, too, the art of the awkward pause). Clayton Corzatte makes the Latin-spouting schoolmaster a rara avis indeed, a lovable bore.

The Leonid Kipnis–Tyrone Guthrie translation is

clear and colloquial, and Tanya Moiseiwitsch's unfussy period sets make the problem of adapting a play written for the proscenium stage seem no problem at all.

Guthrie's *Hamlet* moved with the rhythm of a fist relentlessly clenching and opening. His *Three Sisters* rises and falls like quiet, even breathing. It is compassionate and lovely and I hope that you will see it.

Howard Taubman on **Death of a Salesman** from "The New York Times," July 20, 1963:

How does *Death of a Salesman* stand up more than ten years after its introduction on Broadway? At the Tyrone Guthrie Theater it rounds out a repertory that includes *Hamlet, The Miser* and *The Three Sisters.* Is Arthur Miller's play a classic, like Shakespeare, Molière and Chekhov?

No one can be sure how it will assay fifty or one hundred years from now. Today it is still a compelling and significant drama. As performed by the Guthrie Theater's repertory company last night it held a full house spellbound. It got a few laughs, where laughter was not indicated, but there was no question that its unsparing dissection of the life and times of Willy Loman, traveling salesman, and his family cut deep into the audience.

On re-seeing *Death of a Salesman* one becomes aware with renewed force that the Lomans are a metaphor for the debased values by which so many Americans live, no matter how well-meaning and decent they are. Getting ahead is the great good and it breeds illusions that distort character and deform lives.

Death of a Salesman is the tragedy of a little
man. By the standards of classic tragedy, the strict
constructionists of criticism have told us, the play
therefore cannot achieve greatness, for its protagonist
lacks nobility and does not contend with the fates.

But why worry about classic pigeonholes? What
matters about *Death of a Salesman* is that it anato-
mizes our society, digging to the roots of what corrupts
the Willy Lomans even as it reveals them to themselves.
Willy Loman has no heroic stature, but at the last he
dares to look at himself, and his son Biff summons the
courage to know himself.

In short, *Death of a Salesman* is still relevant,
even in our affluent society—perhaps more so. The
Guthrie Theater was right to present it. Moreover, the
chances are that many of its patrons are seeing it for
the first time.

The production directed by Douglas Campbell
makes a virtue of the open stage of this new theater.
The fact that the play takes place in the mind of Willy
Loman is stressed. His house is merely adumbrated
with a skeleton of stairs and interior with a table and
chairs. A lot of scenery is not necessary.

The human elements are more important, glow-
ingly provided for. Hume Cronyn is a notable Willy,
not large and beefy like Lee J. Cobb, the original
Loman, but cocky and distracted like a confused ban-
tam. He shades from euphoria to despair, from bel-
ligerence to defeat, with striking subtlety. His very
walk reflects his mood. Feeling a breath of hope, he
moves lightly. When the hope fades, he becomes stiff-
legged and his feet seem shod in lead.

As Willy's patient and understanding wife, Jessica Tandy is as fine in her way as her husband, Mr.

Cronyn, is with Willy. Lee Richardson plays Biff with the mixture of inarticulate good will and stumbling intensity he should have, and Nicholas Coster is a smooth, empty, self-serving Hap.

The potentialities and rewards of a repertory company are further exemplified by the permanent troupe's expert performances in the lesser, though not indifferent, roles. No one indeed is less than satisfactory. This company can cope with Arthur Miller as well as with the classics of other centuries.

Minneapolis' First Repertory Season, by Brooks Atkinson in the "Chicago Tribune," September 21, 1963:

After roving the world like a Jovian Johnnie Appleseed, Tyrone Guthrie settled down in Minneapolis last spring for his great theater experiment. (In the Queen's honours list he is Sir Tyrone Guthrie, knight-errant of the stage. In accordance with the stern spirit of Article I, section 9, of the United States Constitution, he will be referred to here as Guthrie, although he can be legitimately dubbed Dr. Guthrie, or even Tony, which is the diminutive of a man six feet five inches high.)

Last May Guthrie inaugurated repertory with a resident company on a platform stage in a fresh, modern theater 1,016 air miles from the economic insane asylum of Broadway.

Everyone interested in the theater as an art has wistfully talked about this sort of project for years. Thanks to the confidence and generosity of the people of Minneapolis, Guthrie and his two associates, Oliver Rea and Peter Zeisler, have made the first decisive step. During the summer they have provided Minne-

apolis audiences with four classics—Shakespeare's
Hamlet, Molière's *The Miser,* Chekhov's *The Three Sisters* and Arthur Miller's *Death of a Salesman.*

Since New York will begin a similar project next
winter with a company that will eventually reside in
Lincoln Center, it may be useful to make a preliminary
audit of Guthrie's first season, which comes to an end
on Sunday. First, the platform or open stage. Is it
really practical? Guthrie believes that it is not really
suited to society drama, like Restoration comedies and
the witty plays of Oscar Wilde.

But the vigorous open stage in Minneapolis suits
all four plays in the first season. It is ideal for
Shakespeare, whose plays in fact are inhibited by the
proscenium stage. The open stage also suits *The Miser,*
which is a harlequinade. Although Chekhov wrote *The
Three Sisters* for a proscenium, the delicate interior
life of the play unfolds on an open stage where a pro-
fusion of props sufficiently defines the scenes. *Death of
a Salesman* is the least successful of the productions.
But the failure is less from a lack of scenery than from
the incongruity of the brisk, skeletonized structure that
supports a second-level playing area upstage. The
style, not the stage, is at fault.

Second, repertory. Everyone has long agreed that
repertory develops the range and sensitivity of actors
and also relieves them of the sterile monotony of
playing one part for months. But, until the skills of the
actors are developed over a period of years, the
repertory system results in compromises. Although
Hume Cronyn is perfectly cast as the irascible miser
and is well cast as the doctor in *The Three Sisters,* he
lacks the stature and broken spirit of Willy Loman in
Death of a Salesman. George Grizzard does not have
enough depth for Hamlet but his petulant army officer

Death of a Salesman

Opened July 16, 1963. Directed by Douglas Campbell.
Setting designed by Randy Echols. Costumes designed
by Carolyn Parker. With Hume Cronyn
as Willy Loman, Jessica Tandy as Mrs. Loman,
Lee Richardson as Biff, Nicholas Coster
as Hap, Paul Ballantyne as Charlie.

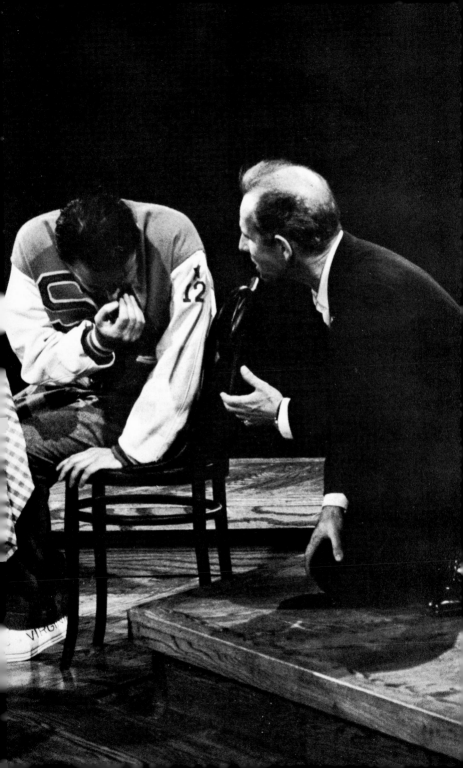

The Miser

Opened May 8, 1963. Directed by Douglas Campbell.
Designed by Tanya Moiseiwitsch. With Hume Cronyn as
Harpagon, Zoe Caldwell as Frosine.

in *The Three Sisters* is admirable. Some of the actors
are well cast in more than one play—Rita Gam and
Claude Woolman, for instance, in *The Miser* and in
The Three Sisters.

During my visit to Minneapolis, Jessica Tandy, in-
capacitated by an accident, played only one of her
three parts. Although her tired, valiant wife to Willy
Loman in *Death of a Salesman* is first-rate, it is possible that she is better cast as Gertrude in *Hamlet* and
Olga in *The Three Sisters.*

Repertory flourishes in theaters, like the Moscow
Art and the Comédie Française, that have long tradi-
tions and—let's not forget—a great many resident
actors to choose from. Meanwhile repertory involves
compromises between perfect casting and the best
casting that is possible at the moment.

In Minneapolis the greatest success this year has
been the audience. It has been not only consistently
large but attentive and responsive. Note, by the way,
that the theater, with its inviting auditorium and wide,
roomy lobbies, has been designed for audiences as
well as actors. We will be lucky if New York audiences
support all the Lincoln Center productions with as much
hospitality and taste.

For what has been happening in Minneapolis
this year has a direct bearing on what will happen in
New York next winter when the Lincoln Repertory company begins in temporary quarters in Washington
Square. Sir Tyrone Doctor Tony Guthrie has cast the
first stone with his familiar combination of recklessness,
confidence and skill.

It is always a pity that dramatic notices teeter
uneasily between being Criticism and being News. Inso-
far as they are News, there is editorial compulsion on

critics to report on the First Performance, and the notice has to be written, and then very probably telephoned to the office, within minutes after curtain-fall. This means that the critics do not have time to digest their impressions at leisure and to have Second Thoughts. It also means that they rarely see a good performance. On opening nights the players are nervous and apt either to be hesitant or to press too hard; and the audience, largely there for the Occasion, is quite unrepresentative of the audiences which the play will thereafter meet. For this reason I include the following notice, written at mid-season.

Hamlet Revisited by John H. Harvey in the "Saint Paul Pioneer," June 30, 1963:

"What a playwright Shakespeare was!" exclaimed my companion.

We were just leaving the Tyrone Guthrie Theater last week after a second visit to Sir Tyrone Guthrie's production of *Hamlet*.

On the face of it that remark might seem a laughable statement of the obvious, but the exclamation expressed a vivid rediscovery of an old truth. Undimmed by all the years, *Hamlet* not only has majesty of poetry, depth and range of human insight and a sweeping sense of the awesome mysteries of this world, but a power to move and excite in purely theatrical terms.

What the Guthrie production of the tragedy does triumphantly is to bring home the fact that Shakespeare wrote both a work of intellectual and esthetic greatness and a whale of a show besides.

All this comes sharply into focus on a second visit to the production; and that is largely because the production itself has now come into clear, steady focus.

Timing, pacing, weighing, proportioning and dramatic trajectory are superb now that all members of the company have relaxed from the tension of the early performances and have come into full rapport with their parts, with each other and with the entire work and Sir Tyrone's conception of it.

It now becomes clear that there is nothing wayward or extravagantly individualistic about the staging, however strange or even shocking some of the business and details mounting may have seemed to some at first.

They are the work of creative genius in clarifying, illuminating and revivifying the director's reading of the text. This reading is penetrating and analytical from a purely dramatic point of view and never goes beyond what is plainly implicit in Shakespeare's words.

And, as one acquaintance remarked in the lobby, "I never realized before how much the old traditional costumes got in the way of what Shakespeare was saying."

George Grizzard's characterization of the title role has grown admirably since opening night. What was careful and even tentative in the early stages of the portrayal has been replaced by greater definition, intensity and bite. There are nuances, accents, flashes of spirit and wit that weren't there before; the sensitivity of his Hamlet is heightened and the agony cuts more deeply.

Ellen Geer's Ophelia has been strengthened, too. The high-school ingénue touches of the portrayal have been eliminated, and she stands forth as a virtuous young woman of spirit and passion. In consequence the sexual flavor of some of her mad songs and accompanying business can be understood simply as expression of natural desire frustrated.

Much the same story can be told about the other cast members in their parts, although I feel that Alfred Rossi and Michael Levin need to rein in their activity as Rosencrantz and Guildenstern. They are both in danger of becoming merely frantic.

To anyone who saw performances of *Hamlet* in the first week or so, my advice is: See it again. You will be gratified at the way the production has grown and matured. And I think you will find, as I did, that it is more gripping and exciting than you imagined that *Hamlet* could ever be.

I do not think that we were too surprised that the lady critic of the "Chicago Tribune" took such a bracingly astringent line. It would have been possible for her to express her disagreement with the interpretations of **Hamlet** and **The Miser** no less clearly but considerably less viciously. And no experienced critic should permit himself the effrontery of "From the introductory plays I can see no company capable of doing much with Checkhov." Retrospective criticism is entitled to be harsh, though not to be rude; damnation in advance is irresponsible; and, in the case of a new and necessarily precarious venture, intolerable.

It is a regrettable fact that it is far easier to write a readable and showy column by being high-coloured, whether in praise or blame. A review which endeavours to be moderate, fair and objective needs to be well-written to avoid being dull. Yet a critic owes some responsibility not just to his readers, nor just to the animals whom he is paid to criticise, the raw material upon which his craft is exercised, but also to himself.

Miss Cassidy is a clever and experienced journalist; and she can write well enough not to need the aid of vitriol. Yet for years her criticism has been disfigured by violent, and often insulting, expression. This kind of criticism is sometimes described as "fearless." I cannot see that it is particularly fearless to hand out strokes of the whip to those whose position makes it impossible for them to retaliate in kind, nor particularly fearless to venture as far as your paper's attorney will permit in the direction of libel, and far further than decency will permit in the direction of wounding, albeit legal, personal remarks. There is nothing to fear except an editorial rebuke; or, possibly, the voice of one's own conscience in the small hours.

8

Audience and Actors

In the first season we played to an average audience of eighty-four per cent of the theatre's capacity. Since matinees and Sunday performances were, during the first ten or twelve weeks of the season, quite poorly attended, the house being sometimes no more than half full, it can readily be appreciated that an average of over eighty per cent implies a large number of "capacity" houses.

It may be that in the first season a number of people came just out of curiosity, just to see what the new building was like; and that these people will not come once the novelty has worn off. This would seem to be a likely supposition if the attendance had been larger at the beginning than the end of the season. In fact, it was the other way around. For the first eight or ten weeks the box office was rather alarmingly sluggish. If it had not been for the very large advance sale of season tickets (over twenty-three thousand before the season opened) the houses would have been very thin indeed. But once the third production—**The Three Sisters**—opened, business picked up splendidly. Thereafter, our problem was not so much to attract an audience as to accommodate the people who wanted seats.

Partly this was because **The Three Sisters** was very well liked; partly it was because now, for the first

time, people began to "catch on" to the idea of repertory, to discover how amusing and interesting it can
be to see in quick succession the same actors in several
very different parts, and the same company in several
very different kinds of plays. Partly, perhaps principally,
the school holidays were now in full swing; tourists were
on the move; our audience was beginning to be drawn
from a much wider area than the vicinity of the Twin
Cities.

I am not sufficiently familiar with the American
scene to be able to assess whether our audience was
predominantly drawn from the upper and middle strata
of society. To me practically all Americans seem to be
wafted about in enormous shiny machines, clad in fine
raiment, and to be exuding a curiously ambivalent air
of material confidence and spiritual anxiety. I cannot
distinguish, as I can in Europe, between rich and poor,
gentle and simple, executive and wage earner. But I
am assured, by those who can make these distinctions
in a Midwestern audience, that our public was drawn
from a very wide cross section of society.

What I could see was that it was a notably and
encouragingly young audience, with a youthful alacrity
and eagerness of response. This was especially noticeable in the case of **The Three Sisters.** We had been
nervous how this play would go before an audience
which could hardly be expected to be familiar with
Chekhov. We need not have worried. After the first
five minutes it was clear that the audience was completely "with it," aware that every amusing remark or
situation had its pathetic overtone, while the pathos
was tinged with absurdity.

I do not mean to imply that this is entirely a compliment to the performers. The actors did extremely

well; but their efforts were complemented by the sensitive and intelligent reaction of the audience. Yet I suspect that this happy conjunction may owe less to the merits of the actors and their audience, and more to the fact that our epoch has now caught up with Chekhov. For sixty years he has been ahead of his time; now his style seems familiar and contemporary. All over the world he is now a successful and popular dramatist. Actors and directors now know instinctively how to interpret his work, whereas until quite recently he seemed a difficult, oblique author who said one thing and meant another, whose characters were at one moment plunged in abysses of "Russian gloom" and, at the next, carrying on with an extravagant gaiety, which seemed at best unsuitably childish, at worst completely schizoid.

I think for its first five or six repetitions our performance was an excellent one. But rather soon it began to fall apart. The actors quickly found just where the laughs came, and bit by bit where at first the audience would just perceptibly chuckle with pleasure, the actors encouraged them to big, hearty guffaws. Similarly, where at first there were only hints and implications of pathos and disaster, there gradually grew up strong, explicit emotional displays. After a few weeks one seemed to be watching a performance of quite another play, a well-made comedy, where strong situations were lubricated by rather obvious jokes.

The audience was still enjoying itself very much; but the actors were enjoying themselves a little too much. I do not blame them at all. They did not intend to wrench the play out of gear by exaggeration. I do not even blame myself. Theoretically, I should have been able to see just when and where these exaggerations were occurring. Had I been able to put a finger on them, there would have been no problem about restoring the performance to its original shape. The actors did not intend to distort it; the distortions were too subtle to have been deliberate. I did call the company together and say that, in my opinion, the performance was losing a great deal of its quality and turning the play into a possibly more effective but certainly less interesting kind of comedy. When asked where, and how, and by whom, I could not say. It was a general impression, which I could not substantiate with instances. In consequence my little lecture fell extremely flat and the performance continued slowly, and still to me inexplicably, to degenerate.

Was it, I have sometimes wondered, the audience which was at fault, rather than the players? Perhaps so. After a few performances, it got around that the play was a Great Success. A Great Success naturally attracts a much larger, but also less discriminating, public than that which comes to a new production, prepared to form its own opinion and not to wait to be told by others that it is a Great Success. Perhaps Chekhov's work is not susceptible to Great Success and demands a rather "special," limited public. I do not think this is the case. The blame for the degeneration of our performance probably rests squarely on my shoulders as its Director. I am afraid that I must have failed to see how the play's subtle magic had been compounded; failed to see, and therefore failed to make clear to the actors, just why it is so very much more than a well-made, run-of-the-mill comedy.

The season was arranged so that there would be nightly performances except on Mondays, with matinees on Wednesdays and Saturdays. It seemed a good idea to play on Sunday, when almost everybody is at leisure, and to let the company have its day of rest on Monday, notoriously the worst night of the theatrical week.

This arrangement did not work well. The Sunday performances, which occurred in the middle of the afternoon, were far the hardest of all to sell. It may be that the Twin Cities have strong objections to what may be regarded as "desecrating" the Lord's Day. We received quite a number of letters, mostly signed by such sturdy guardians of the established order as "Disgusted" and "Mother of Nine," protesting against such desecration, imagining that the poor actors were forced to work seven days in the week and could never get to church. In fact, the time of performance was so arranged that neither actors nor audience need miss morning service nor any evening service, which began after six o'clock.

Perhaps a more probable reason for the poor audiences on Sunday is the fact that in summer so many people either spend the weekend in country places or take off for long expeditions by car. It had been our hope that, while people in the Twin Cities might at weekends depart Elsewhere, people Elsewhere might possibly make an expedition to the Twin Cities to see a play.

Since this hope was rather signally disappointed, we plan in the second season to abandon Sunday performances and to play instead in the traditional arrangement of six week-nights and two matinees.

In the first season arrangements were made with the educational authorities for special performances of **Hamlet** and **The Miser** for high schools. Young people from fourteen to eighteen years of age arrived in busses and seem to have enjoyed themselves. They were a quick and responsive audience and the actors, though they found that the young people's reaction differed from that of a grown-up audience, enjoyed these performances very much.

As a result, both the educational authorities and the theatre management have been encouraged considerably to increase the number of performances. It is our hope that, in addition to welcoming parties of older boys and girls to see classical plays in the theatre, it may be possible to send groups of professional players into the schools to give recitals and demonstrations and performances of material suited to those of tender years.

Gradually we hope that it will be possible to increase the length of our seasons from about twenty weeks to as much as thirty. This, we feel, is probably long enough. It would seem to be wiser not to operate year-round; you are then apt to be taken for granted by the public. The theatre would soon be regarded as something which is conveniently "laid on," like water or electric light.

On the other hand, we should like to be able to offer to our actors year-round contracts. Only so can we expect them to be ready to stay for several successive seasons; and only if a considerable proportion of each season's actors do so stay can we establish the continuity of style and attitude which is an important part of our policy.

To fill the remaining weeks of a year, we would like each year to plan a second, or special, season of rather more ambitious calibre than the main season. While this special season would be available to the general public, it would be aimed primarily at university students. The programme would consist of works which, while acknowledged as masterpieces, are generally considered a little too ambitious, too "difficult" for the ordinary public, and, consequently, are hardly ever professionally presented.

Our plan would be to produce one or two of such works; there would be performances each night, and, in the daytime, preparatory lectures, demonstrations of excerpts and discussions, at a level to be appreciated by serious and intelligent students.

Such a plan would not, we expect, be economically self-supporting, and could only be implemented through the close co-operation of universities. Such co-operation presents obvious difficulties, not merely in the financial department, but in respect of transport, commissariat and especially schedule. University students have their days so closely packed that the time for such a scheme as we propose would be hard to spare.

However, even if such an ambitious scheme as this may take a few years to materialize, we do not anticipate that it will be too difficult to arrange a full year's work for the actors. Already there have been offers from film and television companies. A tour might be arranged. The possibilities are manifold.

Given a full year's employment, we believe that many actors will be willing to stay with the company for several years; and we further believe that the audience will like to know actors a little better than is possible when they stay for no longer than a single season, and appear in no more than three parts.

When the same people work together for a considerable period and in a number of productions, then, and only then, can a company develop real cohesion and a style of its own. We are anxious to develop such cohesion and we believe that this would be of great service to the American theatre, which is probably the least cohesive in the world and in which teamwork, though it is often excellent, never has any chance to develop into a recognizable style of acting or production.

Changes in the company's personnel will be made, for the most part, at the top. After playing leading parts for a season, actors should leave and, one would hope, return again after an interval of a year or two. By this means the promotion in the company will not be gummed up. This year's second line of players will become next year's leading players, and so on down the ladder. New players will then enter the company on the lowest rung, and hopefully work upwards.

Of course, this is putting it all too simply. In practice, second players cannot all be promoted to leading parts in the following year. And one cannot guarantee annual promotion all the way down the line. The factor of personality has to be reckoned with. Second-line players, however technically well-equipped, are not always of the calibre to play "star" parts; or maybe the repertoire will not offer suitable parts to a particular player. Also the regrettable fact must be admitted that the most interesting and exciting actors are not always the most deserving characters; whereas, contrariwise, the most decent and reliable citizens are not necessarily those whom the public aches to see as Lear or Macbeth. Merit, in short, cannot always be the key to promotion.

Gradually—and that may easily imply a process lasting over ten years—we intend that the company shall be more and more indigenous to the upper Midwest. And the key to this will, we hope, be the McKnight Fellowship plan, which enables graduate students from the Drama Department of the University of Minnesota to enter the company.

If in each season, ten or twelve youngsters of exceptional promise enter the company as McKnight Fellows, it ought to be possible to keep three or four of these continuously occupied for several years. In a few years this element, some Minnesota-born, all Minnesota-trained, will begin numerically to dominate the company; and, hopefully, to give it what so few theatrical companies truly have, not merely a "local habitation and a name," but a definably local and provincial style. And here I use the word "provincial" not in the contemptuous sense, in which in these metropolitan-minded days it is customary to use it, but as a term of the highest respect. It can, and it should, imply that those who are "provincial" regard themselves as citizens of no mean city.

All this, it will be noticed, implies the possibility of long-term thinking and planning. This is basic to the whole idea of this theatre.

Now, if there is going to be a systematic attempt to create a definable style, certain steps will have to be taken immediately. The first and most important of these is concerned with the technique of speech.

This is, to my mind, easily the most important element of the actor's craft, as opposed to his art, and one which is much neglected in the American theatre.

Can the reason for this be that there is almost no incentive for Americans to speak "well," and quite a strong incentive to speak as much like other Americans as possible?

In other countries, to speak well is to speak like a member of the upper classes, or to speak as if you had been expensively educated. It must be admitted that there is a strong element of snobbery in either alternative.

In America there is an almost religious abhorrence

of snobbery, and an almost religious belief, although it is in contradiction to easily and immediately observable fact, that the barriers of class distinction were swept away when Independence was declared and have never been allowed to rise again.

This means that it is considered offensively un-American to try to, or even to want to, speak "better" than any of your neighbours. It savours of putting on airs. In most European countries, education authorities put a good deal of emphasis on the correct, and even elegant, use of the native language, both as regards grammar and pronunciation. My impression is that in America the emphasis on all this is considerably less. No doubt this arises largely from the excellent intention of teachers not to make "new Americans" feel different or inferior. And I suspect that a great many Americans make a cult of speaking in a purposefully sloppy way, because so many of their neighbours have but a very imperfect command of the English language. They use a small and rather vulgar, albeit often vivid, vocabulary; their pronunciation is heavily tinged with the sounds of their native language, be it Russian, German, Italian, Mexican, Japanese or Czech. This means that even well-born, well-educated Americans make naïve noises, like "twenny," meaning "twenty"; or "li'l," meaning "little"; or "dreckly," meaning "directly."

Is speech like this appropriate in a theatre which aims to present classical plays with distinction?

I think not. But what is the alternative?

In Britain actors are still taught to speak as members of the upper class are believed to have spoken some years ago. But now the scions of nobility are no longer isolated from contaminations of vulgarity. Even at Eton, the lordlings are compelled to mingle with the sons of tinkers, tailors and candlestick makers, who have crashed the gates on scholarships. One might have hoped that the young tinkers would have picked up ducal accents. But, alas, the vulgar boys are not only more numerous than their betters, but ever so much more clever and lively. It is their accent which dominates. The heirs to dukedoms leave Eton speaking like Eliza Doolittle before she encountered her Pygmalion.

Therefore, the British actors will have to model their speech upon something other than that of the upper orders.

Since radio, movies and television enormously influence the speech of all communities, and since in these media the standards of speech are principally set by actors, perhaps the matter is not without importance. Upon standards of speech, set by the stage, depends the future of spoken English.

Now, while our theatre is not in Britain, the plays are given in the English tongue, and "good" English pronunciation is therefore important.

How shall we define "good" speech?

Currency based upon the "U" standard has, probably for some centuries, been devalued. I assume that in the fullness of time other standards may suggest themselves, as a result of future social and linguistic developments. Are we to wait passively until such developments occur? Had we not better try to create some standards, even if only as a temporary and possibly makeshift measure?

In Germany there is a conscious and successful method of stage pronunciation which avoids sloppy vulgarities, inappropriate to the classic drama, and also avoids the snobbery of being pseudo-aristocratic. Such pronunciation is called **Bühnen-Deutsch.**

I propose to experiment with our company in the creation of a stage English. It will not spring ready-made out of my Anglo-Irish hat, like Athena from the helmet of Zeus. It will be gradually pieced together by communal methods, out of discussion and attempts to take what we believe to be common-sense decisions.

Where communal agreement cannot be reached, a ukase will be issued—by me. Those who refuse to recognise such ukases will be asked to seek work in a more permissive environment.

The ukase will only be issued on clearly definable principles; for instance, "dreckly" will not be permitted as a substitute for "directly," because it omits both a percussive consonant and a syllable, and because it divorces the word from its root, "direct."

Naturally, I shall not try to impose a British style of pronunciation. American English is a distinctive, even dominant form of English. Indeed it is rapidly replacing English English, even in England. There the teenagers, under the influence of film and television programmes, cultivate American accents and styles as laboriously as, sixty years ago, Henry James strove in the contrary direction.

This seems to make it more, not less, incumbent upon those who value the English language to seek, in America, for a native elegance.

Two American members of the company have agreed to act as instructors. They both have exceptionally well-produced voices, have thought a good deal about what constitutes "good" speech, and both speak a lingo which sounds to Americans, as well as to me, entirely unaffected and entirely appropriate in a classical context. They will take classes and "chair" discussions. Out of this, I hope that we may begin to find a unified, dignified but not pompous diction and pronunciation which is neither pseudo-British nor "Mid-Atlantic"; which, while unmistakably American, will avoid the naïveté and vulgarity of much colloquial American speech, and also avoid the least attractive stigmata of English as she is spoke in the upper Midwest—notably an excessively nasal placement and whining drawl.

It may be asked why we propose to rely upon two men, who are primarily actors and only secondarily speech teachers, who are young and have no distinguished experience to give them authority. The answer is that while, no doubt, there must be many such authorities in the United States, we have been unable to locate them. The very few whom we believe to be first-rate are engaged elsewhere; others, who might be available do not seem to us, for one reason or another, to be a better alternative than the two actors whose work we know, in whose technical ability we have confidence, and upon whose tact and taste we are willing to stake the whole attempt.

Quick results are not expected. Mistakes will be made. We must grope our way slowly, and often painfully, towards a goal of whose precise nature we are as yet uncertain. But at least the nettle is being grasped.

A unified and carefully considered manner of speech is, I am convinced, the first step towards evolving a distinctive acting style. It may also, just possibly, be a valuable step in the direction of an attitude towards speech, more sensible than the inverted snobbery of being reluctant to speak better than the neighbours—keeping back with the Joneses.

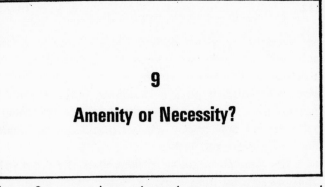

9

Amenity or Necessity?

Almost five years have elapsed since my partners and I agreed, over a Sunday breakfast in New York, to embark upon this enterprise.

It certainly would not be true to say that we have achieved our end, because in this sort of enterprise you never reach an end. You go on and on, like a donkey before whose nose is suspended a certainly subjective and probably hypothetical carrot; on and on you plod, nearly always uphill; and it really does not matter that you know perfectly well that you will never munch the carrot.

But there has been some achievement; and I hope that it will not seem immodest to assess it.

First, the Twin Cities have a handsome new theatre, enshrining a very new, even revolutionary idea.

What is new about it?

Certainly not the programme, which is almost defiantly old, for reasons which have been discussed in Chapter 3. The novelty is that it is operated neither in order to make a financial profit, nor to express the private tastes of a patron, or patrons, nor for the self-expression of its leading artists. It is owned by a non-profit-distributing trust and operated as a public service.

On the continent of Europe there would be nothing new about this. Almost all the serious theatres are owned either by the municipality or the state, and are not expected to make money. The idea has long been accepted in Europe that serious art, be it theatre, music, painting or literature, cannot be expected to pay its way financially. It pays a dividend, it is believed, in making the citizens more "civilised." The same thing is believed not only about art, but about religion, medicine, education and justice.

The English-speaking communities do not expect churches to pay their way, or hospitals or universities or even schools, except a few "private" ones; it is even generally accepted that **some** forms of art cannot pay their way and actually deserve the support of public funds—painting, for instance, through public art galleries; and literature, for instance, through public libraries.

Until 1941 the English-speaking communities offered no public support to the dramatic arts.

In that year it was feared in Britain that, under the threat of war and instantly expected invasion, arts and culture generally would have a hard struggle to survive. It was recalled that in 1914–18 there had occurred a formidable recession in taste. Serious books, plays, music and pictures were temporarily put aside in favour of war-winning activities and relaxations of the most frivolous and often vulgar quality. In 1941, in fear of a repetition of this, there was formed the Council for the Encouragement of Music and the Arts—CEMA in the wartime jargon, which substituted initials for all names, not just for cumbrous ones like this.

CEMA was founded on a grant from the Pilgrim Trust (an Anglo-American foundation) which the British Government matched with a grant of the same amount. It made itself responsible for serious concerts, distribution of paintings and, for the first time in British history, government money was used to support the theatre. The first recipient was the Old Vic, which received a cautious guarantee against loss, in respect of a tour to the coal-mining districts of South Wales. Dame Sybil Thorndike headed a company which played **Medea** in miners' halls for three months, mostly one-night stands.

In fact, the premise upon which CEMA was founded—that the war would be the death of the arts in Britain—was confounded. Under the threat of destruction there was a surprising but glorious rallying of spiritual forces. The people of Britain were not only unshaken by panic, not only put forth a supreme practical effort in the organization against air raids and invasion, the equitable sharing of food and clothing in the face of scarcity and the transformation of the country's entire economy so that war material had priority and so that every able-bodied man and woman was occupied in work of national importance. Over and above all this, there was enough energy left for a remarkable spiritual and intellectual renaissance. Public libraries reported that never before—and, alas, never since—had there been such a demand for serious literature. Music, drama, opera and especially ballet flourished as never before—or since.

This meant that, while CEMA did not prove strictly necessary as a saviour and protector of serious art, it was very helpful and acquired great prestige as a central distributor. It acquired further prestige when, a year or two later, Lord Keynes, the eminent economist, became its chairman. Through his influence it was reconstituted on a less impromptu basis. The government now took over its entire financial support. Considerably increased grants were made available by the Treasury and issued through the Board of Education. The cumbrous and pretentious name was changed to the Arts Council of Great Britain.

At the end of the war its work continued and gradually expanded. The Old Vic, Covent Garden and Sadler's Wells continued to receive financial aid, as did many of the provincial repertory companies, whose work was considered significant, and whose management was honest and capable.

Yet, in case anyone should be considering how artistically enlightened and liberal the British Government had become, it was only in 1963—eighteen years after the end of the war and twenty-three since the foundation of CEMA—that the Treasury agreed to make its grants on a triennial, rather than an annual, basis.

It is as though cautious officials at the Treasury felt that they had been stampeded by Lord Keynes twenty years ago into a dangerous course, which they might regret. In spite of his worldwide reputation as an economist, he was also known as a dilettante, who had married a ballerina. Let us wait a little while, they seemed to have said, before wading deeper into these dangerous waters.

But now the Arts Council and its beneficiaries can begin to plan, if not on a long-term basis, at least on a slightly longer term than before. Hitherto they could never absolutely rely upon Arts Council support for more than a year at a time. From my experience with the Old Vic alone, I can give more than one instance of how cramping and irrational that has been; and, worse, how fatal it has been to count on Arts Council chickens before they were hatched.

Very, very gradually in Great Britain the idea begins to be apprehended that a serious theatre cannot exist on a self-supporting basis; and that perhaps providing the funds to suport a serious theatre may be a responsible way to spend a very limited amount of public money.

In America the idea may, as yet, hardly be said to have taken root at all. There is, as yet, no equivalent of the British Arts Council; should it be proposed, it would be in the gravest danger of foundering between the Scylla of federal and the Charybdis of state aid and authority. Manifestly the wealthier and more populous states could, if they wanted, support their own equivalents of an Arts Council. It is equally manifest that the Dakotas, New Hampshire or Alabama, for instance, could not. Yet this problem, difficult as it may be, would not preclude the possibility of aid for the arts from public funds, if enough people were strongly convinced of its advisability. They are not—for several reasons.

First, the United States is still wealthy enough for extensive private patronage to be possible. The individual patron can still provide subvention for painting, and collective private patronage can still support symphony orchestras and even opera companies.

There are two further sources of patronage more private than public: first, the great foundations created to administer enormous fortunes, of which perhaps the Rockefeller and the Ford are best known. These are not directly controlled by their founders, but they are most certainly not public funds. If you want help from them, you must apply to trustees, and especially to professional secretaries or administrators, who are employed as their almoners by the trustees. These men become, in effect, important patrons in a number of fields, of which art and scientific research are only two. They defend their decisions, if necessary, before their boards of trustees, a very different matter from defending them before Congress, or before a state legislature or a municipal body; the trustees tend to be very much more enlightened, disinterested and highly educated men.

The second area of semi-private patronage is occupied by great business firms, which, from time to time, have enormous funds at disposal and can either make outright gifts, or commission works of art—decorations for their buildings, for instance—or use their art patronage as a means of creating a benevolent public image, or even as outright promotion. Texaco, for instance, has for years given immense financial assistance to the Metropolitan Opera, but not quite in such a way that its right hand did not know what the left was doing.

While these sources of private and semi-private patronage continue, the need for public subvention of the arts will be by that much the less acute.

Then, as regards the theatre especially, there is a widespread belief that if a theatre is well managed it can pay its way; or to put it another way, that a request for subvention is no more than a confession of inefficiency. This belief is a complete misapprehension. In theatrical management there certainly is, as in any business, a traceable connection between insolvency and inept management. But the converse does not hold. An inefficiently managed theatre can make huge profits. The increase in profit caused by efficient, as opposed to inefficient, management is proportionately small. The profits are made by providing highly popular attractions; and I will not accept the proposition that a manager who always seeks for highly popular attractions, to the exclusion of all other considerations, is a good manager. I will not even accept that he is the most efficient kind of manager, since the search for popularity is a highly unscientific, highly subjective, highly speculative matter, conducted entirely by guesswork. No one knows beforehand what will succeed. The best, luckiest and most experienced managers are being continually confounded. Those who make fortunes do so, not by making a high proportion of correct, or lucky, guesses, but either by making an enormous "killing" out of a very few lucky guesses; or else, like Mr. Merrick, by creating a sales mechanism which can make money even out of a flop. But this, while it is in many ways to be admired, can hardly be called theatre management. Merrick's productions are often erratically and chaotically managed. The bacon is brought home by merchandising techniques which have no exclusive connection with the theatre but could be applied equally to the sale of soap or beans or face powder.

The reports of the enormous profits to be made out of a successful Broadway production have created an illusion that the so-called "commercial" theatre is indeed a viable commercial operation. Of course it is nothing of the kind. A combined balance sheet of all the productions in New York during the course of a single year, during the last twenty or thirty, would show the most devastating losses. Broadway is the most highly subsidised theatrical operation in the world.

Since even the "frivolous" theatre, a more accurate description than "commercial," requires subvention, it is hardly surprising that a "serious" theatre should do so too. A serious theatre makes more demand upon its audiences' concentration, and supplies less of the trappings in the way of glamour. It is not, however, at all true to suppose that the entire serious theatre is either opposed to, or unable to achieve, glamour. In so far, however, as it makes heavy demands on concentration it cannot hope to scale the peaks of popularity. These, since we are all lazy most of the time and many of us lazy all the time, are reserved for what can be assimilated with the absolute minimum of exertion. This is why commercial television is as it is.

What reasonable arguments are there against public money being available for a serious theatre?

The best, I think, is that public money ought not to be wasted and that the theatre, whatever its artistic pretensions, should not be regarded as anything but a luxury and a frivolity, upon which luxurious and frivolous people may, if they like, squander their own money, but not that of the taxpayer.

Can the theatre reasonably be regarded as no more than luxury and frivolity?

Can it reasonably be regarded not just as an amenity but a necessity in a community which wishes to consider itself civilised?

Of course the theatre is not a necessity in the same category as bread and water and elementary sanitation. Life can be supported without a theatre.

But communities rather soon outgrow the stage where necessities are confined to that which just supports life. Rather soon the term "necessity" begins to be applied to that which renders life interesting as well as supportable. At a very early stage of civilisation, self-expression becomes a spiritual, if not a physical, necessity.

I am not an anthropologist, and I cannot grade in a logical order the amenities which gradually become necessities in a developing society. But it is clear that play, and especially playing at make-believe, becomes indispensable at quite a low level of development. Incidentally, it is also noticeable how playful animals are, and that more intelligent animals are more playful than duller ones.

In all human societies, telling and listening to stories has been one of the principal sources not only of pleasure but of instruction. The most vivid way of telling a story is by means of impersonation. Drama is just that: the re-creation by actors of a group of persons and a series of events. Great drama always adds to this some philosophical comment or allegorical overtone, not necessarily—or even frequently—with a conscious didactic purpose, but always with didactic possibilities. For example, in **Oedipus Rex** of Sophocles, it was almost certainly not the author's purpose to offer a little homily upon the virtue of simple piety, nor a cautionary tale against parricide and incest; nor even, as many of the greatest commentators have suggested, against getting too big for one's breeches. It may, more probably but by no means certainly, have been his intention to present an allegory about children and parents. Few can doubt that it was his intention to make his wonderfully told story something more than the thrilling tale of detection which, among many other things, it also is. Its greatness may perhaps be just because its meaning is so mysterious. Any intelligent spectator at a good performance of **Oedipus Rex** cannot help but feel that it has something very important to say and very personal to each one of us, but no one has yet been able to contain this meaning in an explanation which is at once simple, plausible and interesting.

Clearly in this instance we have come a long way from the games of tag played by monkeys, hide-and-seek by cats, or peekaboo by infants of the human species. Yet in all drama the traces of these simple games remain. You can clearly see the traces of hide-and-seek in **Oedipus Rex,** and all other detective plays. Tag is a dominant influence in all Westerns, all dramas which involve chasing and catching. What else is peek-aboo but a primitive form of the actor's entrance and exit? And what else are entrances, exits and games of peekaboo but primitive allegories of birth and death?

The point is that while, admittedly, all drama is play, all play is not necessarily either a frivolous or a primitive manifestation. It is not insignificant that we speak of the "play" of intellect, and the "play" of imagination, or, perhaps most strikingly of all, the "play" of light. If Galileo had not permitted himself this kind of "play" we should still be assuming that the sun moves round the earth.

Of course, the particular forms of play which occur in the theatre carry a considerable load of sexual association. It must be freely owned that the theatre has assumed a good deal of responsibility for sexual stimulation and sexual instruction, which in other cultures is assumed by religion; but which, sometimes for excellent reasons but also sometimes with horrible results, the Christian Church has abrogated. It was not always thus. Up to the end of the Middle Ages the Christian Church was the great distributor and patron of drama in Europe. It is ironic that, after the Reformation, both the Old Church and the so-called Reformed Church were united in a Puritan condemnation of the stage. Very possibly the stage at this time, like the monasteries at the time of their dissolution in Britain by Henry VIII, was asking for trouble. It is to be regretted in both cases that reform was not more temperate and discriminating.

Puritan disapproval of drama has lasted especially

long in America. I have been fascinated to find how widespread and how strong is the belief, even among quite well-educated and apparently sophisticated people, that the theatre is a licentious exercise in sexual provocation; that actors are, each and all, "no better than they should be"; that the few who survive sexual contamination nevertheless lead a pitiably silly life, "painting their faces and showing off."

This, more than any other single factor, explains, I believe, the general reluctance to regard the theatre as being in the same category as other more respectable forms of art, literature, painting and music; and the absurd pretence that drama—which is so obviously "great" that not even the severest Puritan can suppress it—should not be enjoyed as it was meant to be enjoyed, on the stage, but should rather be "studied" as literature.

It would be idle to pretend that the Puritan case has no validity at all. The theatre **is** a powerful sexual stimulant; and constantly **has** turned, and still frequently **does** turn, this power to cynically mercenary ends. But the power is not always misused; and the stimulation is not always "dirty."

Nor is it honest simultaneously to chide the theatre for misuse of great power and to dismiss it as childish frivolity. Nor is sexual excitement the only powerful stimulus which the theatre can exert. It is also, and often simultaneously and just because it is sexually exciting, a powerful awakener of other ideas. I do not pretend that all these ideas are "good." That would be as silly as the Puritan, who tries to maintain that the yare all "bad," except where, here and there, they may tend to support his own rigid and narrow convictions.

An idea which seems "bad" to me may seem

"good" to you. Am I therefore justified in trying to shield you from contamination by this idea? Or justified in the still more extreme measure of suppressing such an idea? Why should I assume that I know better than you what is "good" or "bad"? And how dare I assume that what may indeed be "bad" for me must therefore be "bad" for you?

Now if the theatre is admitted to be a powerful source of ideas, bad as well as good, then there is an unanswerable case for organising a theatre which will propagate acceptably and powerfully what its organizers regard as good ideas. There is no case at all for suppressing the theatre, as Puritans have always tried to do; or, when that proves impossible, to try to kill it by bitter and intemperate disapproval. There may be a case, though I cannot see much reason in it, for the present state of laissez-faire in which the theatre is allowed to survive only if it pays its way; that is to say, only when the ideas which it offers, be they good, bad or indifferent, are popular.

So much for those who would suppress the theatre as a source of powerful and dangerous and "bad" ideas.

Now what about those who would dismiss it as mere frivolity?

It is hard to see how the medium for which Aeschylus, Sophocles and Euripides wrote could possibly be so dismissed. It is hard to see how the work of Shakespeare can be so dismissed. One would hardly accuse Racine or Corneille of frivolity. Molière, under a mask of frivolity, grins like a wolf, while he snarls and snaps at vice and folly. Ibsen in his time has been accused on a formidable list of counts; frivolity was not one of them. Eugene O'Neill, Arthur Miller, Tennessee Williams, Lillian Hellman, Clifford Odets and Thornton Wilder are Americans whose names are known and respected all over the civilised world. Their reputation was not earned because of their frivolity.

The accusation can, I admit, be applied justly and forcibly to a high proportion of the Broadway offerings in any given season. But these are almost all mere baubles offered for sale in the entertainment market; they make no pretence to be anything but frivolous, and they have almost nothing whatever to do with a Serious Theatre. To condemn the theatre as a whole on their account is like condemning all shoemakers as rogues and cheats because some cheap shoes let in the rain.

In general, the accusation of frivolity comes from people themselves too ignorant to have heard of Aeschylus or Ibsen, or too frivolous to have bothered to find out what they are about. Or else from people who cannot believe that an activity is "serious" unless it produces tangible results.

This last attitude is prevalent amongst people who, probably justly, regard themselves with pride as good business men. The serious purpose of life, as they see it, consists in creating Things, or moving Things from place to place, or buying and selling Things. This, not unreasonably, they regard as a Service to Mankind and, as such, worthy of respect and reward. The best of them are not unduly eager to be rewarded and are sincerely and humbly eager to be of service. But is it not possible that they hold a rather limited and rather over-practical view of what is serviceable?

To many splendid citizens of this kind, art and culture are merely frills on the garment of life, appropriate occupations for the leisure of rich women. Here and

there, they will admit, a great genius may appear—a
Beethoven, a Leonardo, a Shakespeare—whose work,
they will admit, has been widely influential. But the
odd great genius, who may also be expected to be a
great Nut, and probably rather an "unstable type"—
wasn't Leonardo a homosexual?—absolutely does not
justify sensible people in wasting their time on something unproductive and, maybe worse, unconventional.
Such self-indulgent nonsense does not forward the Serious Business of Mankind.

Too often one hears statements like this: "I began
with nothing but the two hands on the ends of my arms.
I left school at eleven. I'd never read a line of Shakespeare. I didn't know Yankee Doodle from the Marseil-
laise. The only pictures I ever looked at were in the
mail-order catalogues. But look at me! Worth half a
million before I was fifty. Mayor of the City. And now
a Senator."

What does this prove? That Shakespeare, Leonardo, Mozart and all that lot are useless? Or merely
that they are not indispensable aids to getting to the
top of a highly materialistic heap?

So long as society remains highly materialistic,
and so long as getting to the top remains a very respectable—even the most respected—notion of how to
behave, then speeches like the foregoing will carry
some weight. But what would Plato have made of a
speech like that? Or Jesus Christ? And somehow it
would seem better sense to attempt, however feebly, to
derive one's ideas from one or both of them, rather than
from the Chamber of Commerce.

All the same, if you do think it extremely important—and the point of view is certainly not silly, and in
certain contexts can be admirable, even noble—to con-

tribute to the material betterment of society, then Practical Affairs will probably seem to you a great deal more important than Art or Culture; and your attitude will seem only more rational to you, not less, if you have a considerable natural aptitude for practical affairs and have been conditioned by every important influence in your life to regard culture as a pretentious, long-haired bore. In such a case you will probably not be very receptive to the argument that the Material Betterment of Society would be accelerated, not retarded, if the cultural standards of society were rather higher; that imaginative people are not necessarily idle drones, that they have indeed a higher practical potential than the less imaginative, provided that their practical and imaginative faculties can be successfully combined.

In that case, I must play—reluctantly, because it implies a bleak outlook—my ace of trumps.

Each year machines are now doing more of the work which was formerly done by humans; not only mechanical diggers and drills and shifters to relieve us more and more of exhausting physical drudgery, but also calculators to do a great deal of the clerical work—the adding, subtracting, measuring, sorting and copying—to say nothing of a great deal of deciding.

Foreseeably, there are going to be fewer and fewer jobs; and the least skilled, the least privileged and the least bright will, as always, be the first to go to the wall. While there will be many fewer jobs and many, many persons unemployed, it would not be reasonable to suppose that the jobs of most of those who will still be employed will become more interesting;

quite the reverse. Most of them will be engaged in the deadliest of repetitive tasks, a routine of operating the machines. There will be a comparatively small élite of highly skilled mechanics, who will mend the injured machines and make new ones to replace those which wear out. And above them a smaller élite, who will plan the machines' work. And above these, next only to God, an even smaller élite, who will regulate the policy of industry, who will determine, aided more by mechanical calculators than by their own five wits, what is made, and where, and why.

Presumably if society is not to disintegrate entirely, we shall cushion ourselves against the most violent shocks. Instead of throwing millions of workers completely out of employment, we shall try to arrange that more people work for shorter hours. If the work has to be fairly shared, so will the pay. All this will involve painful practical re-assessments and re-adjustments. But maybe we can make them without too much violence and misery.

But the practical re-adjustments will be nothing compared with the philosophical ones.

For countless generations we have been taught that man must live by the sweat of his brow, and we have interpreted this as meaning the sweat of his body. That interpretation is ceasing to have meaning. In the future man will not sweat physically except as a matter of recreation; but if he is to survive, he will have to do plenty of intellectual overtime.

Work will no longer be a penance undergone for the sake of the pay envelope. If we are not careful, it will be the longed-for, probably fought-for, anodyne against the unendurable boredom of leisure.

Although technically we have abolished slavery, except in out-of-the-way corners of Africa and Asia, we have nevertheless morally enslaved immense sections of our apparently free societies. Most of us spend the greater part of our waking lives in deadly drudgery, often for very high wages; but the recipients of such wages rarely have either the leisure or the energy or the education to spend them very wisely or productively. Even those of us who, either by ability or inherited wealth, are not condemned to drudgery are for the most part self-condemned to a slavery hardly less base. We are the slaves of convention. We hardly think for ourselves at all. We imbibe through mass media the ideas and the ideology of the Chamber of Commerce. We think it of paramount importance to wear the right clothes, eat the right food, send our young to the right school, have the right car, the right vacation, and, finally, the right interment. In every case, "right" means that which our social group endorses. If suddenly the "right" thing should turn out to be "wrong," all of us would be frightfully disrupted, and most of us totally lost.

But this is exactly what is beginning to happen. The foundation of our whole way of life is that we are here to work. It is assumed that it is not only the serious purpose of our existence, but the basis of material reward. And this assumption has continued for so many generations that it is now part of a social order which we take for granted; the disruption of this will invalidate a whole complex of associated preconceptions.

The formidable thing is that the pace of the changes will probably not be controllable. To survive economically whole groups of industry will have to be mechanised as fast as possible. We see it occurring now in coal and steel. We see the beginning of it in clerical work. There is every reason to suppose that the pace of the change will be accelerated. The mechanised firms will produce faster and more cheaply than those which still employ human ants. It will therefore be "mechanise or bust." Whereas, in order to make the social and spiritual adjustments less painful, it is desirable that while the inexorable need to mechanise be accepted, the pace of the changeover should be retarded.

How does all this relate to the theatre?

It is difficult to doubt that over the next generation or two, millions of people are going, whether they want it or no, to have an immensely greater amount of free time than they have had previously. It is going to be a question of paramount importance how they spend it. Either it can be spent in a manner which will expand and improve our human powers, or it can be spent, as is so much free time at present, in a search for ever greater physical and spiritual comfort. At present only an exceedingly limited section of society is trained to make intelligent use of spare time. The preconception is that energy should be reserved for work; and that leisure time should be used to rest, in order to build up a new supply of energy for further work.

This preoccupation has some meaning in primitive conditions, where almost all work makes great physical demands—digging ditches, felling trees, ploughing, sowing and reaping. It even has some meaning in highly complex societies, for those who are called upon to make great efforts of dexterity and concentration— surgeons or scholars—or to face the nervous strain of great risks—seamen, truck drivers or merchants. It has almost no meaning for those who have to perform the monotonous routines of the Assembly Line, where the demands made on physical, intellectual or nervous energy are minimal.

Since their work is dull and undemanding, workers in this last category ought, you might think, to use their leisure creatively, and take advantage of their considerable spending power to this end. The evidence, however, is that, in general, these are the members of society who make the least intelligent and energetic use of their leisure. They have not shaken off the inherited preconception that the serious purpose of their lives is to work; and that how they spend their leisure is of comparative unimportance either to themselves or to society. For two or three generations now, the overwhelming majority of the more affluent communities have been employed in routine and undemanding industrial tasks. But this fact has not shaken in the slightest degree the preconception that it is these ant-like services which entitle them to material reward and the respect of society.

It is what people **are,** not what they do or what they are **paid,** which is important.

In this connection the term "culture" must be drastically re-assessed. In our currently materialistic society practical achievements have been overestimated and over-rewarded. Achievements of the mind and spirit have been correspondingly undervalued. In America this is because a complex and affluent society has developed so very quickly out of the simple and Spartan society of Pioneering Days, when practical achievement was an absolute necessity of survival and when there was very little time or energy for other kinds of achievement. In consequence the term "culture" has come to be regarded—erroneously—as having very little to do with practical achievement, and to be used in an almost entirely pejorative sense.

In fact, we can none of us escape culture. We are the product of it. There are, of course, considerable

differences between the culture of a Central African
native and that of Park Avenue; and much smaller differences btween Park Avenue and the Lower East Side,
or Park Avenue and rural areas of the Midwest. There
are even smaller differences between the culture of
well-off, highly educated persons and that abstraction,
the Average Citizen.

It is one of the dangerous features of modern life
that these comparatively small differences are exag-
gerated, so that a wide gulf seems to separate "cultivated" people from "ordinary" people. The gulf seems,
I believe, much wider than it really is because of mutual
snobbery. "Cultivated" people stress the inanity of
"popular" taste; deplore the low level of commercial
entertainment, the vulgarity of tourist centres like Miami
Beach and Las Vegas. They do so with an offensive air
of superiority, and this, not unnaturally, is resented by
the people who like "pop" art and Miami Beach. This
resentment expresses itself in jibes at the expense of
culture, which is taken to be the equivalent of snobbery
and "snootiness"; and about which "ordinary" people,
in their turn, become "snooty" and snobbish.

It is time that both sides appreciated more gener-
ously that neither is quite in the right and that the gap
which separates the two is not as wide as it might appear. Ordinary people who think that "culture" is solely
for blue-haired ladies had better think again; had
better realise that they are themselves the product of
an extremely elaborate culture going back for thousands
of years. This culture has been formed not only by what
thousands of previous generations **did,** but equally by
what they **thought** and **felt:** in short, by what they **were.**

"Cultured" people had better realise exactly the
same thing. Culture is not just a matter of reading

Proust and Joyce and collecting ancient bronze. That is all **part** of our culture; as is riding on the subway, saving the harvest, listening to sports results on the radio and having glorious fun with pinball machines at Atlantic City.

Until we accept that everyone, literally everyone, is part of human culture, and is himself, at however primitive a level, a Cultured Person, we have not begun to grasp either the meaning of the term or the possibilities of the human race. And until we accept the fact that it is snobbish and silly to classify one kind of culture as "higher" than another we are only widening an artificial and very dangerous rift in society.

I am not pretending that I do not think Beethoven's music "higher" because I find it more interesting, elaborate, varied and original than that of the average Top Ten; nor Proust a better writer than Grace Metalious. I think so because I have had certain educational "advantages." But it would be idle to pretend that these have not totally unfitted me to understand many important ideas and to perform many useful functions. In other words, "high" culture in one department is achieved at the expense of others; no one can be "fully" cultivated.

But all of us could be more fully cultivated and achieve a better-balanced culture, given the opportunity. The principal obstacles to such opportunity hitherto have been, first, the interior one of our own inertia; second, the exterior factor, lack of leisure as a result of economic pressure.

Leisure for all is now within our grasp. Can we overcome our inertia?

People are inert for physical and moral reasons. Physical inertia is usually a matter of bad health, often due to inadequate diet. This is an economic and medical matter and not relevant to this argument. But inertia is not less frequently a matter of boredom; of not wanting to make an effort because one's interest has not been aroused. Art is an important factor in the conquest of this kind of inertia. It exists to make people more interested in themselves and their environment by showing things about themselves and their environment which they would not otherwise have been able to see.

When an uninstructed person looks at a field he sees simply a mass of not very interesting or various material, mostly green. When a farmer looks at the same field he sees an infinity of shapes and colours and textures, all of which have associated meanings. The field to him becomes a book full of lively significance.

So it is with art. Nearly all of us have some small affinity with art. We like a nice tune, or a pretty picture. But we do not go much further. Consequently music or pictures do not afford us either a very varied or interesting experience.

I do not think, however, that there is anyone who does not like a good story. For most of us sustained pieces of fiction or history demand too much concentration. But is there anyone who can resist a really juicy piece of gossip, or a sensational newspaper report, especially if it is sexy?

Drama is the telling of a story in the most vivid possible manner. Therefore it has always been a very popular, very generally appreciated form of art. But it is not always necessarily an easy art to enjoy, because it makes heavy demands upon the concentration of its audience. Most dramatic performances last between two and three hours, and that is rather longer than many people can concentrate. And to enjoy a play it is necessary to give to it your uninterrupted concentration. You cannot, for instance, relax for a few moments, as you can when reading a newspaper or a book, and then go on to read some more; you cannot go at your own pace—the pace is set by the actors, and you have to keep up with them.

Partly because of these heavy demands, being a member of an audience can, when the performance is good, be a uniquely thrilling experience. This, I believe, is because it provides a stretch of the imagination, exactly analogous to the use of the muscles in physical exercise. A well-exercised and disciplined imagination will be capable of more effort than a slack one.

This, over and above mere pleasure and relaxation, is, I suggest, the point of going to the theatre. It offers a unique intellectual and emotional stimulous. If you respond, then you will be giving your intellect and emotions a stretch. Is such a stretch desirable? One is always hearing old ladies say about serious plays: "I'd rather see something amusing, dear. There's enough sorrow and misery in real life without going to the theatre to see more." Perhaps this is a just point—for sad old ladies. But the sorrow and misery of a tragedy are entirely different from those of real life, partly because you are a spectator not a participant, but more because it is presented in an orderly and significant form and offers some comment upon the events and emotions portrayed.

The old ladies really mean that they want to go to the sort of play which involves the least possible effort. And again for sad and tired old ladies this is, no doubt, right and proper.

But is this a right and proper attitude for vigorous, healthy people? It is at present customary to tolerate an

old-lady attitude in vigorous people when it is applied
to leisure. But this tolerance depends upon leisure being
regarded as no more than a relaxed period of play between bouts of strenuous work. When work either
makes no energetic demands or becomes a scarce
luxury, then our energies, if they are not to atrophy,
must be applied to activities which at present seem to
be no more than play.

I do not think that it will be too hard to persuade
people that a part of their leisure should be spent in
physical culture. There will be greater difficulty in per-
suading them that equally great efforts must develop
their intellect and imagination. This is where the arts
in general, and the theatre in particular, have a greater
responsibility than ever before for the safety and health
of mankind.

This is where a serious theatre becomes a necessity, not a luxury.

And this is why it seemed to us when we embarked
upon this project that our theatre must not operate for
private profit, nor as a toy for private patrons or artists
in search of self-indulgent expression. It seemed important that it should be constituted and regarded as a
public service.

And so it has been constituted: it has been built by
public subscription, and is operated for the community
by fully professional actors and staff. The management
is employed by a trust and can be changed if unsatisfactory. But the trust is responsible solely for the
theatre's general policy and does not take decisions in
respect of programme or casting or administration, beyond an over-all approval of each season's budget. The
theatre is neither a business, nor part of an educational
institution. It has, as I have endeavoured to indicate, a

long-term policy, concerned with establishing a classical repertory company, with strong local attachments,
aiming gradually to achieve its own distinctive style.
The purpose of all this is to be of some use to the American theatre at large, where neither artistic cohesion nor
an attitude to the classics are strong suits; but, especially, do we aim to be of use to the community which
has called us into being and supports us.

Here let me once again emphatically disclaim any
idea that our aim is to Improve people, to Do them
Good. We are there to offer a selection of plays of
proven worth, performed at the best standard which
we can achieve.

Whether they have an improving, an uplifting
effect, is the business of the audience. One person may
be uplifted by **Hamlet,** another be downcast. And, just
as we do not regard it as our business to be improving,
so we do not regard it as our business to Educate.

The theatre exists to entertain. Entertainment can
be educative; but it is a regrettable fallacy that a serious theatre must be consciously instructive. The fallacy
has been fostered by theatre people, because we have
learnt, by bitter experience, that public bodies will give
you funds if they can be persuaded that you aim to
Educate. But if, more truthfully, you admit that your
first aim is to Entertain then you won't get a cent. It is
part of the good, old preconception: Work, including
education for Work, is serious. Play, including even the
most serious entertainment, is not serious and therefore
not educative.

But, if it is agreed that the wise use of our leisure
is important, then not only does it become necessary to
take play seriously, it had better also be serious to
educate people to play. In short, the idea that enter-

tainment should be no more than pastime is danger-
ously out of date.

It is true that we propose to offer a "serious"
programme, in the sense that plays will be chosen which
have been found over several generations to say something serious to an adult audience. But seriousness must
not be confused with solemnity nor sadness. It is possible to be, as Chekhov, Molière or Shakespeare are,
simultaneously serious and funny.

It is also true that a serious programme has considerable didactic possibilities. There is much wisdom to
be learnt from a close acquaintance with, let us say,
four plays of the calibre of **Hamlet, The Miser, The Three
Sisters, Death of a Salesman,** even when, as is inevitable, the performance is less than perfect. But it does
not therefore follow that the intention of the performance is to teach. He that hath ears let him hear, as
Somebody said, when he told a simple but stunningly
good story, which most of the audience may have
taken at its literal value but which to some others may
have had the allegorical overtones which have made it
immortal.

10

Coda

And now to sum up: Our Theatre has been called into being to serve the community of the Twin Cities. It is our belief that this service can best be rendered, for reasons which have been discussed, by a classical programme; but a classical programme which includes representation of American plays which have not had time to stand the test of survival, but which now seem at least possible candidates for classical status.

All these plays will be given a fully professional performance at the highest standard which we can achieve.

In time, it is our hope that the Minnesota Theatre Company may develop a distinctively Minnesotan style. This cannot come about quickly. It may take ten years or even twenty. The progress will, we hope, be aided by the inclusion in each season's company of a group of graduate students from the University of Minnesota. This is our taproot into the soil.

It will be our aim not to uplift or to instruct, but to entertain, to delight. A good performance of a great play cannot, in our view, fail to instruct. But this should not be the conscious aim of its interpreters, any more than it has been that of its authors.

It is our belief that a programme of this character should not, and need not, be aimed at a cultural minority. It demands a considerably greater **effort** on

the part of the audience than is demanded by a programme of "pop" music or by the average commercial
movie, which is deliberately and condescendingly
aimed by its makers and promoters at a hypothetical
intellectual and emotional level lower than their own.
This kind of condescension, though it is often commercially successful and possibly even commercially necessary, leads, in our view, to artistic death. An artist is
entitled to assume that his public is less interested and
less sophisticated than himself in his particular field. He
is not entitled to assume that his public is, in general,
less intelligent or sensitive than himself; or that well-off,
well-educated people are more intelligent and sensitive
than others who have not enjoyed the same advantages.

An experiment of this kind simply cannot be judged
in short term. It is essentially an attempt to apply
longer-term policies and a more serious, though not I
hope on that account pompous, approach to the theatre
than is implicit in the frantic pursuit of the Smash Hit.

Naturally, this does not mean that every member
of every audience is not entitled to a severely critical
attitude to every performance, as well as to our whole
policy. Without such an attitude a theatre can be killed
by kindness, like an overstuffed pet dog.

But criticism of particular faults can be made with
a patient and favourable attitude to the whole endeavour. This project is something more than the sum
of a number of disparate productions and performances, more than the expression of a group of particular
personalities. It is an attempt to relate a theatre to its
supporting community. If such an alliance is to be fully
fruitful, then patience, tolerance and forebearance are
going to be demanded of all parties.

In America particularly, but increasingly in the

whole modern world, an apparently (though not, I think, really) accelerating pace of change creates a demand for quick results. Every institution, like every animal or plant, has its own normal rate of growth. Good results are constantly being frustrated by the silly impatience of people who want to accelerate the natural pace. A theatrical institution can only be created very slowly. Many errors will be committed, many misdirections will be followed. The character of the institution will only form very slowly, and far more by a process of spontaneous growth than by the fulfillment of the conscious intentions of its founders.

Nonetheless, there must be such conscious intentions. This project has come into being through four years of hopes, which then became intentions, which then became practical decisions. Until, at last, a theatre was built, a company assembled, performances given. Finally, an audience came to see these performances and gave many signs of enjoying them very much.

It is our hope that gradually, as audience and management become mutually better acquainted, the audience will begin to create the sort of theatre which it wants, which will be an expression of itself.

Only thus can the intention of this project be fully realised. It is much more than merely building a theatre and creating a series of productions. The ultimate aim is to attract a creative audience.

The three greatest periods in the history of the theatre—the Athenian stage of Aeschylus, Sophocles and Euripides; the Elizabethan stage in England which produced Marlowe, Shakespeare, Ben Jonson and half a dozen lesser but significant poets; the French stage of Racine, Corneille and Molière—all these could not have happened if the writers, actors and craftsmen had not been fortunate enough to live in an age and place where a highly intelligent, lively and demanding audience had helped to create a theatre which was far more than a commercial business and far more than a frivolous pastime. Neither the artists and craftsmen nor the audience can do this alone. It is a shared process of creation, a fruitful union.

In sum, our project is to set up conditions where such an union may eventually be possible. No one can predict exactly how this new kind of theatre will develop. We must all keep open, but not therefore empty minds. It is all too easy for those who work in a theatre to be disproportionately puffed up by success and cast down by failure; and, as a result, to pursue too eagerly a popularity which is ephemeral and often achieved at the cost of eventual reputation. It is all too easy for the audience of a theatre to take an irresponsible view of its share in the creation of standards; to assume that "support" is enough, without regard to the quality of the support.

That attitude belongs to an era when the theatre was organised as a business and where the public had no more responsibility than a purchaser of merchandise. Those days are ending. If a particular public wants to have a serious theatre it must undertake the responsibility not merely of a customer but of a patron. That involves the exercise of Taste.

The development of taste is not just a matter of sensibility. Taste is formed by experience. That is why at Minneapolis we are starting with a classical programme: to enable an audience to form its taste by contact with what the best minds of several generations have agreed to regard as important expressions of the human spirit.

Later on, when both the management and the audience know better what we can and ought to attempt, and also what we can and ought to afford, then we may take the risk of producing, and possibly commissioning, new work.

The greatest works of art have, almost without exception, been created to please intelligent and sophisticated patrons. The greatest works of drama have, almost without exception, been written with a particular theatre, or particular public and a particular group of actors in mind.

When, and if, our theatre can offer the right kind of conditions to a writer, or a group of writers, then we may begin to expect interesting and contemporary results. Meantime we believe that we can slowly begin to create such conditions.

Our policy may seem to many people more conservative than they would like. We must risk their disapproval; we must creep before we can walk. If our progress seems too deliberate, let me ask you to recall the result of the celebrated sporting event when the Hare raced the Tortoise.

Index

About the Author. For seven years, Tyrone Guthrie was managing director of the Old Vic and Sadler's Wells, and in 1952, he was called to Stratford, Ontario, "to give advice" when the now famous Shakespeare Festival was being organized. In addition to his work in the theatre, Sir Tyrone has written plays and has contributed to numerous publications in Europe and America. He has lectured at colleges around the world, including Oxford, Cambridge, Yale, Harvard, Melbourne, and Sydney Universities. Harold Clurman, director and critic, has called him "the most gifted director on the English-speaking stage."